African Apocalypse

THE STORY OF NONTETHA NKWENKWE, A TWENTIETH-CENTURY SOUTH AFRICAN PROPHET

Robert R. Edgar and Hilary Sapire

Foreword by Shula Marks

Ohio University Center for International Studies
Monographs in International Studies
Africa Series No. 72
Athens

Witwatersrand University Press
Johannesburg

Published in the Republic of South Africa
by Witwatersrand University Press,
1 Jan Smuts Avenue, Johannesburg 2001, South Africa
ISBN 1 86814 337 6
© Robert Edgar, Hilary Sapire 1999

The books in the Center for International Studies Monograph Series
are printed on acid-free paper ∞

05 04 03 02 01 00   5 4 3 2 1

Cover photographs: Elders of the Church of the Prophetess
Nontetha in prayer before the commencement of the
exhumation of Nontetha's grave *(Anton Hammerl)*;
and *(inset)* Portrait of Nontetha, painted by Lizo Pemba

Library of Congress Cataloging-in-Publication Data
Edgar, Robert R.
    African apocalypse : the story of Nontetha Nkwenkwe, a twentieth-century South African prophet / Robert R. Edgar and Hilary Sapire ; foreword by Shula Marks.
        p.   cm. — (Monographs in international studies. Africa series ; no. 72)
    Includes bibliographical references and index.
    ISBN 0-89680-208-6 (pbk. : alk. paper)
    1. Nkwenkwe, Nontetha, ca. 1875–1935. 2. Church of the Prophetess Nontetha Biography. 3. Women prophets—South Africa—Eastern Cape Biography. 4. Prophets—South Africa—Eastern Cape Biography.
I. Sapire, Hilary. II. Title. III. Series.
BX7071.Z8N594   1999
289.9'3—dc21
    [B]   99-16273
                                                              CIP

Contents

Illustrations

Foreword

This book is about an extraordinary story of discovery. Or rather three such stories. The first is the story of the remarkable prophetess Nontetha, an uneducated Xhosa woman who, in the aftermath of the influenza epidemic which ravaged the eastern Cape after the First World War, preached that a day of judgment was drawing nigh and exhorted her followers to unite. A second story is how Nontetha was unjustly incarcerated for thirteen years in South Africa's notorious hospitals for the insane and the grim story of psychiatric care in twentieth-century South Africa. Finally there is the amazing story of the discovery of Nontetha's bones in a pauper's grave in Pretoria and their return to her still devoted followers in the eastern Cape.

These stories truly represent multiple excavations. Until Robert Edgar discovered Nontetha's descendants and the Church of the Prophetess Nontetha some twenty years ago in the course of writing his doctoral thesis on the more famous Israelite church and their massacre at the hands of the South African police at Bulhoek in the eastern Cape, the story of Nontetha and her followers was as buried from public view as Nontetha was in her unmarked grave. As Megan Vaughan has remarked, "For the most part . . . the voices of the mad cannot be heard by us at all. Historians of Africa search constantly for the authentic 'African voice' in the colonial archives and find it hard to uncover. Hearing the authentic voice of the mad African in written documentation really does involve straining the ears."[1] Thanks to Robert Edgar and Hilary Sapire's work of excavation, we no longer need to strain quite so hard.

Nor was the twentieth-century history of psychiatric services in South Africa much easier to uncover. Most of the unpublished government papers on psychiatric care in South Africa in the first half of the century have been destroyed, while in the late 1970s it became a criminal offense to publish material on conditions in mental hospitals. So Sapire's work on psychiatry in South Africa was equally dependent on excavation. As this remarkable volume shows, Nontetha's incarceration "occurred at a key moment in the history of both psychiatry and in the consolidation of segregationist thought and practice" in South Africa and thus "provides a unique window onto the world of mental hospitals and psychiatric practice" in the inter-war years. Edgar and Sapire have given us one of the very few texts to illuminate this world in twentieth-century South Africa.

Finally, and in a very material sense, the return of Nontetha to the burial grounds of her ancestors was the result of careful scholarship and actual excavation. Not the least moving section in this book relates Edgar's efforts to locate and exhume Nontetha's remains and their ceremonial reburial in the context of a post-apartheid South Africa coming to terms with its melancholy history. Her present-day followers are among the many black South Africans currently tracing their disappeared dead.

Ever since the publication of Foucault's classic, if flawed, *Madness and Civilization*, the history of madness has attracted scholars who have recognized that the history of the most marginalized in society can be used to illuminate a far wider canvas. Thus, in his study of the history of mental asylums in colonial Nigeria, Jonathan Sadowsky has remarked that "colonial asylum policy reveals in microcosm the dynamics of the Nigerian colonial state." Sally Swartz has argued more widely: "The mixture of liberal humanist medical practice, universalising psychiatric knowledge and naturalised racism and sexism in colonial contexts became the web within which colonial tensions were expressed. For these reasons to study the management of the insane in the colonies becomes a history of the tensions of Empire in a more general sense."[2]

Nontetha's prophecies, so revealing of the power relations in the colonial state, "threatened," in Megan Vaughan's suggestive phrase, "to disrupt the ordered non-communication between ruler and ruled."[3] At a time when the eastern Cape was shaken by the defiance of the millenarian Israelites, Nontetha's prophecies seemed particularly ominous. Suspected of sedition, she was committed to Fort Beaufort Mental Hospital in 1922 and then transferred to the Pretoria Mental Hospital in 1924. There, cut off from kin and community, she died a "lonely and painful death" in 1935, and, despite the best endeavors of her followers to have her body returned for appropriate burial, was thrown into an anonymous pauper's grave.

Nontetha's case would seem to vindicate those who argue psychiatry's function of social control especially in the colonial situation. And undoubtedly, as Edgar and Sapire remark, mental hospitals and psychiatry have their place "in a continuum of disciplinary and custodial institutions, such as prisons, migrant labor compounds, and reformatories," which served South Africa's industrializing order. Yet they are equally careful to point out that Nontetha's incarceration was the exception rather than the rule, the product of its timing rather than an intrinsic aspect of South Africa's technologies of controlling dissent. Indeed, they contend, ironically it was probably her gender which protected her from the fate of male prophets who were considered subversive, and who were dispatched to the even more brutal jails of South Africa. Throughout the twentieth century, South Africa can be more readily indicted for confining the insane in its bleak prisons than for incarcerating its political opponents in its overstretched mental hospitals.

There are further ironies in the state's interpretation of Nontetha's prophetic vision as madness, however. Colonialism had after all brought the evangelical and millennial Christianity she espoused to the African continent. In many ways her prophecies fitted well with an evangelical belief system which went beyond the rational, which ultimately saw man's soul as constantly engaged in a cosmic struggle between God and Satan; religious ecstasy and divine insanity have long been intertwined in Christian theology and experience. In indigenous cosmology, too, divine inspiration and the inspiration of divining were arrived at after a period of "madness." Had Nontetha rejected the message of the colonizers and remained with that cosmology, there can be little doubt that her fate would have been very different. Although this volume illuminates what I have termed the "separate worlds we all inhabit, but which are made more frightening and separate by the divisions of age, ethnicity and race," paradoxically it also illuminates the connections between those worlds.

Wisely Edgar and Sapire refuse to speculate about Nontetha's mental condition and clinical diagnosis. Regardless of pathology, Sadowsky has reminded us, we need to read the records of the colonial "insane" with "the recognition that resentment and aggression are predictable in a colonial society." Africans and Europeans in colonial contexts had "different cognitive realities not only because they had different cultural backgrounds"—important as they were—"but because their view of the colonial situation itself differed."[4] What disturbed the South African authorities was not Nontetha's "madness" but her insight.

In the introduction to his *A Social History of Madness*, Roy Porter has remarked, echoing E. P. Thompson:

Posterity has treated the writings of mad people with enormous condescension. Either they have been ignored altogether, or they have been treated just as cases. But it would be foolish to fly to the other extreme and try to turn the mad *en bloc* into folk heroes, into radicals and rebels. It would be mistaken and terribly sentimental to rush headlong into concluding that the voice of the mad is the authentic voice of the excluded, that somehow madness leads the chorus of protest against dominant elite consciousness, indeed sings the song of the repressed.[5]

In this account of the story of Nontetha, however, Robert Edgar and Hilary Sapire have discovered a subject who was indeed leading a chorus of protest against dominant elite consciousness; if not singing the song of the repressed, she was, as Edgar and Sapire carefully suggest, providing "a haunting accompaniment to the many dreams of and cries for redemption and renewal outside of the asylum walls."

SHULA MARKS

Acknowledgments

This study was researched and written in several stages, beginning its life in 1974 as part of Robert Edgar's Ph.D. dissertation on the Israelite Church and other millennial movements in the eastern Cape and Transkei in the years following the First World War. After coming across fragments of the story of Nontetha in several government files in the State Archives in Pretoria, he followed up by locating the Church of the Prophetess Nontetha in the eastern Cape and interviewing two of Nontetha's children and several of her principal followers. However, because the main government files on Nontetha were not yet open, he concluded there were too many gaps in her story. He put off writing a full account until the mid-1990s, when, in unexpected ways, his and Hilary Sapire's academic interests converged. Shifts in both South African politics and historical writing, notably in gender history, the cultural history of medicine and healing in southern Africa, as well as a renewed interest in the history of Christianity and conversion, prompted a fresh consideration of Nontetha's life.

In the early 1990s, Hilary Sapire began research into the social history of psychiatry in South Africa. While scouring the state archives in Pretoria for sources on mental institutions in twentieth-century South Africa, particularly for the voices of their African inmates, she was alerted by fellow historian Catherine Burns to the existence of several bulky files in the Native Affairs Department's records. These contained fascinating evidence on the incarceration of a Xhosa woman prophet, Nontetha, in mental hospitals in South Africa in the 1920s and 1930s and led to the discovery of additional files in the archives of the Justice Department and the South African Police. After establishing our mutual interest in Nontetha's life, we decided to pool our resources. What started out as an extended essay has blossomed into this much longer study.

During the course of our study, we have incurred many debts to colleagues and friends in South Africa, the United States, and Britain. First, we would like to acknowledge the cooperation of the Bungu family, especially Dumalisile Bungu, the late son of Nontetha, and Nontombi Bungu, the late daughter of Nontetha, whom Robert Edgar interviewed in 1974. The Bungu family as well as leaders and members of the Church of the Prophetess Nontetha have long supported the writing of the history of Nontetha and her church. Reuben Tsoko, a founder and head of the church, and his successor, Mzwandile Mabhelu, have especially welcomed our initiative. Both in 1974, when Edgar first met church members and Nontetha's family, and then in 1997 and 1998, we both experienced their warm hospitality and were inspired by their enthusiasm for our project. Our meetings with them continued to influence the shaping of this book. For instance, in August 1997 they presented us with a key source, a handwritten account in isiXhosa of Nontetha's visions and dreams and her followers' treks to Pretoria. This document added considerably to our understanding.

In its many guises and phases, academic colleagues and friends have cast their eyes over our manuscript, listened to our seminar presentations, posed sometimes impossible questions, and offered invaluable insights and information. In particular, we would like to express our thanks to William Beinart, Iris Berger, Joanna Bourke, Catherine Burns, Catherine Campbell,

Jim Campbell, Harriet Deacon, Saul Dubow, Deborah Gaitskell, Albert Grundlingh, Manton Hirst, Karen Jochelson, Douglas Johnson, Jeremy Krikler, Paul Landau, Shula Marks, Iona Mayer, Zakes Mda, Sean Morrow, Vuyani Mqingwana, Luyanda Msumza, Jeff Peires, Nokwenza Plaatje, Terence Ranger, Jonathan Sadowsky, Christopher Saunders, A. M. S. Sityane, Timothy Stapleton, Molly Sutphen, and Sally Swartz.

Our colleagues and friends also offered support in countless ways. Alex Mouton kindly photocopied material from the State Archives in Pretoria and sent it to us. Dorothy Porter supplied a steady flow of references in medical history. Felicity Swanson provided information and insights from her own research into the history of mental health care in the eastern Cape. Ros Tatham made copies of newspaper reports from the British Library. Luyanda ka Msumza played a critical role mediating between officials in the eastern Cape provincial government, church leaders, and the Bungu family after the discovery of Nontetha's grave in Rebecca Street Cemetery in Pretoria. Johan Green of Rebecca Street Cemetery assisted with locating the register that contained the entry for Nontetha's burial and arranged for the surveyors that pinpointed her grave. Denver Webb, Ndumiso Gola, Similo Grootboom, Sitati Gitywa, and especially Nosabata Morley of the eastern Cape government's Directorate of Museums and Heritage Resources were tireless in their efforts to facilitate the exhumation and reburial of Nontetha's remains and acted as a vital link between ourselves, the Bungu family, the church, and University of Pretoria academics. The Museums and Heritage Resources Office's commitment to creating a new public history and to commemorating hitherto unacknowledged episodes of the South African past has certainly inspired us. Professors Phillip Tobias and Trefor Jenkins of the Departments of Anatomy and Genetics, respectively, at the University of the Witwatersrand generously advised us on the bureaucratic hurdles that had to be overcome to expedite the exhumation and identification of Nontetha's remains. Professor Maryna Steyn and Coen Nienaber of the Department of Anatomy of the University of Pretoria were the lead scientists exhuming and identifying Nontetha's remains and securing the permits for Nontetha's exhumation. We appreciated the sensitivity and care that they and their archaeological team brought to the exhumation and returning her remains to her home. Dr. Leandre Gauchè, the senior medical superintendent of Weskoppies Hospital, gave us a tour of the hospital and unearthed early photographs of the institution and its staff, which we have used in this book. Sandra Rowoldt and Cecilia Blight of the Cory Library at Rhodes University patiently addressed our research inquiries and identified relevant photographs. Helen Hopps's fine editorial eye and probing questions were invaluable in the final phases of writing this manuscript. Lizo Pemba painted the portrait of Nontetha that appears in this book. Because there are no known photographs of her, Pemba relied on the descriptions of two persons who had known her and one of Nontetha's granddaughters whom the Bungu family says closely resembles her. The *South African Historical Journal* has given us permission to reprint chapter 5, "Dry Bones," which appeared in the May 1999 issue of the journal.

Finally, we both acknowledge the financial and other support given to us by our respective institutions. Hilary Sapire's research was supported on two occasions by Birkbeck College Research Grants as well as a grant from the University of London's Central Research Fund. Robert Edgar's original research in 1973 and 1974 was supported by a Fulbright Doctoral Dissertation Research Fellowship. His research in the 1990s was funded by the Institute of Social and Economic Research at Rhodes University, the Office of the Vice President for Academic Affairs at Howard University, and a Fulbright Faculty Research Award.

Introduction

One of the goals of a modern police state, wrote Hannah Arendt, is to "establish holes of oblivion into which all deeds, good and evil, would disappear." She exhorts us "to preserve history and civilization by descending into these holes, rescuing those individual deeds and recounting them to ourselves and our children."[1] In the past few years, the darkness of South Africa's "holes of oblivion" have been daily revealed through the testimony to the Truth and Reconciliation Commission, and through the mosaic of stories of those whose lives have been touched—often broken—by the series of grim deeds perpetrated in the name of apartheid. Illuminating these holes of oblivion is an essential political and human act; only when the terrible legacies of apartheid and the longer record of colonialism are fully apprehended can the more recent transformations be understood and an authentic reconciliation begin to be achieved, writes one historian.[2]

Among the many stories that are being recounted in this period of reflection and recasting the past is that of Nontetha.* It begins in late 1918, when for three terrible months, the world's most devastating influenza epidemic tore through

*We have used the spelling "Nontetha" throughout this book because it is the spelling preferred by her descendants and the Church of the Prophetess Nontetha in recent years. This spelling conforms to changes in Xhosa orthography adopted in the 1930s. However, government officials in the 1920s and 1930s and Nontetha's followers as late as the 1970s spelled her name "Nonteta" (or other variations).

southern Africa, leaving hundreds of thousands of people dead in its wake. In its aftermath, many revivalist and millenarian movements sprang up as survivors in black, white, and Coloured communities sought meaning in the calamity and an answer to why it had been visited upon them. While these movements burgeoned throughout the region, they had a special resonance in the eastern Cape and the Transkei. Here, in the heartland of South Africa's first colonial encounters, prophetic figures interpreting the meaning of European conquest and domination had been a prominent feature of the nineteenth-century wars between Xhosa chiefdoms on the one hand and European settlers and British troops on the other. Now, once again, prophets had appeared in a crisis, assuming many guises and bearing a variety of messages of resistance, redemption, and renewal.

One such prophet was an unlettered, middle-aged Xhosa woman by the name of Nontetha ("someone who speaks a lot"). She, too, had contracted the dreaded virus, but miraculously survived. A series of dreams revealed to her that the influenza had been a punishment from God and that she had a special mission to reform her society. It was her duty to preach the Bible to the uneducated, to warn that Judgment Day was imminent, and to stress the unity of the African people.

She began proselytizing in the rural areas around King William's Town, Middledrift, and East London, but just as her movement appeared to be gathering strength, the Bulhoek massacre of May 1921 occurred. Nearly two hundred members of the Israelite church were killed in a showdown with police near Queenstown. White anxiety about the recurrence of "Bulhoek" created a highly charged atmosphere, and the authorities detained Nontetha on two separate occasions for what they called seditious activities. From 1922 until her lonely and painful death in Pretoria Mental Hospital in 1935, Nontetha was severed from her immediate kinfolk and family and kept in jails or mental hospitals. However, her devoted disciples were undeterred by her incarcerations. They nurtured the movement she inspired and sought to bring her plight to public attention in a dramatic 600-mile "pilgrimage of grace" from the eastern Cape to Pretoria.

Despite the fact that her following never rose to more than a few hundred and that she was sequestered in the narrow confines of penal and mental institutions for many years, the compelling story of her life and her fate at the hands of the authorities touches on and helps elucidate a number of important themes in the social, political, and cultural history of South Africa.[3] For example, her own midlife conversion experience and her establishment of an independent Christian church among non-Christian, unschooled peoples speaks to a renewed scholarly interest in conversion and the history of Christianity in southern Africa. Moreover, the details of her life and mission prompt fresh reflections on the problematic relationship between resistance and religious "madness" in a colonial situation.

Interrogating the conflicting views between Nontetha's followers and the psychiatric establishment as to her mental state raises questions about a series of critical issues. One is the general cultural and political gulf between Africans and whites, as well as the divisions within both societies. Another is the role played by mental hospitals and psychiatry in the regulation of South African society, and their place in a continuum of disciplinary and custodial institutions—such as prisons, migrant labor compounds, and reformatories—which served the industrializing system so well.[4] While the documentary record of the country's mental hospitals is incomplete, the traces there of Nontetha reveal much about the power exercised by psychiatrists, magistrates, policemen, and state officials in the everyday politics of the first three decades of this century. These records thereby offer us a tantalizing insight into what Fred Cooper and Ann Stoler call "the stretch between the public institutions of the colonial state and the intimate reaches of people's lives."[5]

The very marginality of figures like Nontetha in popular and academic writing about African protest and resistance reflects the extent to which the existence of African prophetic and millennial movements, and their relationships with more orthodox nationalist and worker movements, have largely been neglected. As a consequence, in most standard accounts the wide variety of ideological and cultural strands that have been entwined in the making of modern African identities and politics remains hidden.

If the apparently dead-end, deluded imaginings of millenarian visionaries have not as yet found their place in the historical literature of African resistance, neither have the "voices of the mad," despite the fact that they offer eloquent commentary on the most common sources of discontent within African societies, as well as a haunting accompaniment to the many dreams of and cries for redemption and renewal outside the asylum walls. The voices of the mad are also acutely revealing of the day-to-day concerns and of the micropolitics of the wider society. The inmates of Pretoria Mental Hospital in the mid-1930s, for example, articulately communicated to a visitor their resentment at pass laws, land dispossession, and police brutality and the collective experience of the overwhelming majority of Africans in that period.[6] It is important to "get inside the heads of the mad," writes one historian of madness. "For one thing, their thought-worlds throw down a challenge, being at once so alien yet so uncannily familiar, like surrealist parodies of normality. For another, if we are to understand the treatment of the mad, we must not listen only to the pillars of society, judges and psychiatrists: their charges must be allowed a right of reply."[7]

Nontetha's story is also a constant reminder of the gendered character of social experience. This is a continuous thread running through all these themes and issues. Nontetha's story richly evokes the role of female independent Christian and prophetic movements in rural African life, particularly in regions such as the Ciskei. In such labor-exporting areas, the prolonged absence of men contributed to the fundamental reshaping of relationships of gender and generation and affected every facet of economic, social, and cultural life. Moreover, her gender was to be a critical variable affecting the attitudes and responses of both the state and psychiatric authorities to the conundrum that Nontetha presented. As we suggest, it was precisely because this intractable prophet was a woman that she was stigmatized as mad and incarcerated in a mental hospital.

Finally, as we were completing this study, we had our own experience with peering into a hole of oblivion. When Nontetha died in 1935, state officials buried her in an unmarked pauper's grave in a Pretoria cemetery and refused to hand over her remains to her family and followers. In 1997 we were able to locate her grave. At the behest of Nontetha's descendants and the Church of the Prophetess Nontetha, and with the cooperation of eastern Cape provincial government officials, we participated in the successful exhumation and return of her remains to her home in October 1998. The involvement in this enterprise of family, church, government, and academics raises important questions about public history and memory, how future histories of South Africa are to be recorded and commemorated, who the custodians of the past are, and the relationship of professional historians to the creation and production of history. Although we may not be able to address all these issues fully in this study, they should challenge all of us involved in the recording and retelling of the South African past.

African Apocalypse

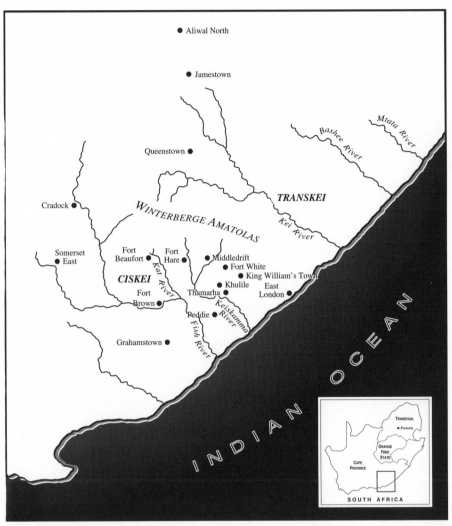

Eastern Cape

1

Isibeto

And he said, "Hear my words: If there is a prophet
among you, I the Lord make myself known to him in a
vision, I speak with him in a dream."
                                        —Numbers 12:6

Prelude to Prophecy

The facts about Nontetha's life before she launched her
prophetic career are sketchy, but they point suggestively to
wider trends taking shape in her region. She was born about
1875 and grew up in Toyise location, an imiDushane Xhosa
area near King William's Town, as a century of ferocious war-
fare between Dutch and British settlers and Africans in the
eastern Cape was entering its final chapter.[1] Nontetha's area
bore the brunt of many of these wars. European colonizers
were ultimately the victors; they sliced swaths of land away
from African chiefdoms and compressed their peoples into a
reserve between the Kei and Keiskamma rivers that came to
be known as the Ciskei. The aim was twofold: to create a buffer
zone from African societies to the east and to provide a source
of labor for Europeans. Those who collaborated with the
British, such as the Mfengu and Gqunukwebe, were rewarded
with land grants. Those who resisted, such as the Ngqika and
Ndlambe, lost good portions of their land. In Nontetha's area,

it did not matter much who collaborated or who resisted because Mfengu, Gqunukwebe, Ngqika, and Ndlambe were all squeezed into adjoining patches of land.

During and after European conquest and the creation of African reserves in the Ciskei and Transkei, an increasing number of people were unable to sustain a living from the land, and they became part of the diaspora of African migrant laborers forced to seek work on European farms or in urban centers throughout South Africa. Since the majority of migrant laborers were male, the reserves were increasingly populated by the aged, women, and children.[2] This imposed enormous emotional and economic stress on women, who already had multiple responsibilities—child care, planting, hoeing, weeding, and harvesting crops and carrying out household chores such as fetching water and collecting firewood and grass for thatching roofs. Now they had to take on even more responsibilities for maintaining their families and homesteads, in situations where they were often extremely vulnerable.[3]

Nontetha was one of the women caught in this predicament because her husband, Bungu Nkwenkwe, left his village of Khulile to find employment, first at Kimberley and then at Saldanha Bay, where he died. As a widow with ten children to raise (five of whom survived to adulthood), Nontetha undoubtedly found herself and her family in precarious circumstances on many occasions.

Another challenge faced by Nontetha was that she had no formal education and spoke no English. In the second quarter of the nineteenth century, mission societies, especially the Wesleyan Methodists, began establishing stations and schools in the eastern Cape's African areas. Because of the spread of mission schools, a schism developed between the "school people," or *amagqoboka*, and the "reds," or *abantu ababomvu* or *amaqaba*.[4] The school people embraced Western clothing, cultural practices, and education; and they distinguished themselves by speaking the English language and participating in the cash economy of the Europeans. The reds, on the other hand, clung to their traditional dress and language and rejected formal schooling as well as resisting participating in some elements of the cash economy.

Figures for the numbers of Christians and non-Christians in Nontetha's area are scant. For instance, the few statistics we have for the King William's Town district tell us that in 1881 reds outnumbered school people by a 4-to-1 margin and that in 1958 reds comprised about 45 percent of the population.[5] However imprecise, these figures indicate the relative balance of power between the two camps and that more and more people were converting to Christianity. And, in such areas, the dividing line in terms of cultural practices was not so rigid.

Indeed, Nontetha did not fit totally in either camp. According to her family and followers, she held no animosity toward Westernized, educated Africans; and her daughter recalled that her clothing included Western dress. She regarded Western education as beneficial and encouraged her children to acquire some schooling at least. Although she never formally joined a church, clearly she was exposed to Christianity, and most of her children were baptized in the Wesleyan Methodist Church after the First World War.[6]

Before she launched her prophetic career, Nontetha had acquired a reputation in her area as an herbalist *(ixhwele)* and a seer. One of her principal assistants, Reuben Tsoko, recollected: "She used to help us a lot when we were boys. We could not be attacked unaware because even if there were boys we had trouble with, no one could ambush us because Nontetha sensed it and informed us. As a result of that, she was even termed a diviner. But she was not a diviner and I think that was the beginning of her being a prophetess. . . . She used to say nothing came at random."[7]

Tsoko's distinction between herbalists and diviners is significant, as is the fact that some were confused about her precise function. As a herbalist and seer, Nontetha would have been a woman of some standing. Ordinarily herbalists in Xhosa society had a "knowledge of a vast array of plants, roots and other substances" and limited their practices to treating physical ailments—such as abdominal or respiratory disorders— or warding off evil influences through protective medicines. A diviner's *(igqira)* purview was wider and included monitoring the health both of individuals and of society by diagnosing the causes of misfortune and affliction and rooting out evil forces. Diviners were especially attuned to the ancestors, who it was believed benevolently looked over their descendants, but who could also bring misfortune to those who practiced witchcraft or neglected customs. Due to the close relationship an igqira maintained with the ancestors, he or she could also be an innovator and initiator, invoking the authority of ancestral inspiration or a special knowledge of medicines.[8]

When someone was struck down by an affliction that could not be treated with the herbalists' pharmacopoeia, that individual, together with friends or family, would consult an igqira to find out why the ancestral spirit was intervening.[9] In the presence of the afflicted, and his or her relatives and friends, the igqira would beat a drum and chant *"siyavuma"* (we agree, or we consent). The process of divination varied considerably; sometimes it was necessary to sacrifice goats and cattle or prepare feasts and dances before ancestors would reveal their secret will.[10] Similarly, a spectrum of diagnoses existed that ranged from sicknesses caused by the curse of a living person to ones provoked by ancestral fury.

However, only specialists—*izanusi*—were qualified to diagnose *ukuthwasa* (lit., "to become visible"), a condition signifying that the sufferer had a calling to become an igqira. Citing an example of "a young man, . . . who is noticed to be acting in a strange and unusual manner," the Xhosa historian J. H. Soga describes the steps typically taken by the sufferers and their family: "The signs indicate a serious state of ill health. For long periods, it may be days, he absents himself from home, and avoids contact with other people. Naturally under such conditions he is without food. Later he returns home, and takes to his bed, refusing to hold converse with his people. It is realized then that the case requires the attention of the diviner. This having been discussed, and an agreement reached on the matter, a number of friends set out as a party for the diviner's place of residence."[11]

Trances, dreams, or violent outbursts were signs that the patient was in the early stage of "becoming visible." The calling was revealing itself, and the novitiate had begun. Treatment included the thwasa dance *(xhentsa)*, in which novices and some of the attending igqira are transported "into a hysterical state; some begin to tremble and weep, some faint, others begin hiccupping. . . . Confession is equally important. The novice is exhorted to confess everything she sees in sleeping or waking dreams, so that she may recover. The dancing and confessions are essentially therapeutic for the novice herself: they are part of the cure for *thwasa*."[12] Generally the process of "becoming visible" involved a dream about a plant or fierce animal, which would thenceforth become the healing symbol of the initiate. Accepting the sickness, the symbolism of the dream, and the calling it portended—often after initial resistance—was the first step toward becoming a full-fledged igqira.[13]

The significance of this for Nontetha's biography is twofold: first, as we shall see, Nontetha's experiences before she took up the mantle of prophet resemble accounts of ukuthwasa in some respects and thereby hint at the extent to which Nontetha drew on both Xhosa and Christian sources in defining her prophetic role. Second, given her subsequent incarceration in a mental hospital and transformation into the object of psychiatric scrutiny, it is worth noting that in the accounts of some contemporary observers, notably whites and some "Westernized" Africans, the very symptoms of "becoming visible" themselves were described in that classic psychiatric term— hysteria. B. J. F. Laubscher, superintendent of Komani Mental Hospital in Queenstown during the 1930s, held the view that conditions like ukuthwasa represented psychoneurotic symptoms, which rural Africans simply lacked the capacities to identify.[14]

As an ixhwele, Nontetha was conversant with part of a wider set of healing practices that, as many writers have noted, was directed at curing not only physical symptoms, but the wider societal ills they might symbolize. As such, they were considered part of politics, kinship, and religion—in sum, the culture. Healing also served the further function of interpreting changing realities and finding answers to new questions. In 1918, this task challenged healers and religious figures throughout southern Africa, as the scourge of influenza struck at practically every community, attacking established beliefs and practices and demanding new responses.[15]

Isibeto

Nontetha took up her calling shortly after the cataclysmic pandemic (known in isiXhosa as *umbathalala*, or "disaster") ravaged the region, leaving an estimated quarter of a million dead in its wake.[16] When umbathalala struck the Ciskei and Transkei reserves in mid-October, the death toll was especially high. Although official estimates of deaths were imprecise, the mortality figure of 99.88 per thousand for the districts in Nontetha's area—Middledrift, Keiskammahoek, and King William's Town —was the second highest in the Cape Province and the Transkeian Territories.[17] Influenza was a merciless leveler, leaving few families or communities untouched. As the poignant lines of Reuben Caluza's song put it, "Beautiful daughters, handsome sons, bonny babies, engaged girls, and newly married couples passed away"—usually within a few days of contracting the disease.[18]

Routine activities ground to a halt as people tended to the ill or tried to fend off the fever themselves. Household chores were neglected, cattle were left straying in the fields, and untended crops withered. A missionary in the Keiskammahoek area observed the dead "lying in the same hut as the living, who are, themselves too weak and too indifferent with pain, to try to move them . . . cattle, sheep and goats straying, unherded, and no one to secure the milk, so badly needed, from the uneasy cows; hundreds dying from sheer hunger and exhaustion."[19]

Nontetha's region had witnessed tragedy before, but no war, army action, or police brutality; no government law or proclamation; no drought, famine, flood, insect plague, and animal disease since the cattle-killing episode of the 1850s, wreaked as much human carnage as "Black October." The tremendous loss of life knocked societies off their moorings. Communities looked to their healers and spiritual leaders for answers to fundamental questions: why had the calamity happened and what message did God and the ancestors want to convey?

In the influenza's aftermath, a government-appointed commission took stock of its origins and its impact. At the commission's hearings in East London, testimony adduced a variety of reasons for the extremely high death rate, particularly in the Ciskei, pointing to the lack of nutritious food and medical personnel in the rural areas, poor sanitary conditions, and an unseasonable cold snap. These conditions were aggravated by a severe drought that lasted for many months.[20]

The explanations proffered by commission witnesses did not coincide with the way Nontetha comprehended influenza. She understood the epidemic in other terms. According to her,

God had unleashed umbathalala as *isibeto,* a punishment for people's sins. To achieve salvation, they had to make a dramatic change in their ways. Her revelation came in a series of dreams she had soon after her own bout with the flu.

Her followers recount the most important dream in this way.[21] She had been purchasing mealie (maize) meal from a trading store so she could prepare *imbara* (beer) with her friends to make extra money. Normally she bought the mealie meal on credit and paid for it later with her earnings. As she started brewing the beer, she remembered that she had left a door at a friend's house. She fetched the door and placed it on her head, but on her way back home, the weight of the door grew burdensome. She got a terrible pain in her back and had to bend over until she thought her back would break. When she reached home, she put down the door and was immediately overcome by an illness.

As she lay in bed, she had a vision of two men from above who appeared to her. They asked if she knew them but she did not. Then she saw two doors in her house, one old and one new. She agreed to leave with the strangers, and they exited through the new entrance. They traveled through the sky to the west, where the sun sets, and came upon an open gate that led to a path that went below the earth. They followed the path to several areas where she observed various scenes that "appeared in another country that was green and its grass was cut as if by another machine. As they were strolling about they saw some huts for girls who were preparing for womanhood and some for boys who had been circumcised. She was asked if they recognized the country, and she said she did not. The strangers told her it was Tembuland." Then they went up into the sky again, and she was told to look down on the earth, where she saw a gathering of people viewing the corpse of a young man. Another young man was talking about how the other had died, and he related that Nontetha's husband had died in the same way.

Several messages were conveyed in Nontetha's vision that became the cornerstones of her prophetic message. At one point she observed something wrapped in a dirty cloth hanging from an *umnungumabele* (*Xanthoxylon capense* or knobwood) tree. It had words inscribed on it. She was told it was the Bible, but was rotten because it had not been followed. Nontetha asked Jesus for a piece of the Bible so she could testify on earth, and he told her, "No, we have already given the Bible to people, but they have neglected it." She was to be the catalyst for a new civilization that was coming.

Nontetha was also shown a bag containing a yellowish-brownish concoction, *bubuti*, a medicine used in witchcraft. Seeing it conveyed the message that witchcraft had to be eradicated.

Nontetha and the strangers moved to a place where an unseen person told her that because people were not praying, their sons were dying in the gold mines, where poverty had forced them to work. Women had to share the blame because they were brewing the imbara the young men drank. They were to stop making it because the smoke from brewing imbara had polluted heaven. For this reason, God chose Nontetha, a woman, to preach.

Nontetha was also commanded to visit the great places of chiefs and their counselors and preach to them. She had to instruct them to work together and to ask if they were ready to be liberated and rule their country according to their own ideas of nationhood. The time had come for people to examine their lives critically and give up blaming Europeans when things went wrong.

Finally she heard another voice telling her that the influenza was just a taste of what God was bringing. A judgment day in which everyone would be flying in the sky was imminent. The voice asked her whether people were going to heaven or hell? Her thoughts immediately went to her child who had died in Cape Town during the influenza and to her other children who had died. The voice questioned her: "'What are you going to do today because Doomsday has come?' When I looked up at the heavens, I found them shaking just like the face of a cruel man. When the sun had risen above the earth in the east, it was red like burning charcoal. There was a person inside the sun and he was shaking his fists. And the heavens were coming together and I became afraid and cried. And there was a voice that said to me I should not cry but pray."[22]

When Nontetha came out of her deep sleep, she thought that she had been dreaming. People were hovering over her, holding her hands and splashing water on her. People kept asking what was wrong with her, and she wondered what was happening. Then she realized she had died and returned to life.

Once she recovered fully from her illness, she shared her visions with other people, but they laughed at her. Then she fell ill again, and a voice told her the only way to get better was to wash in a river. So she instructed her eldest daughter to bathe her. When water from the river was poured on Nontetha, she felt healed. She likened the experience to wearing a robe and asked that new dresses be removed from a box. At this moment she claimed she had been specially robed and endowed with unique powers.[23]

Nontetha's illness and her dream both incorporate Xhosa beliefs and tenets and Christian symbols. The account of how she was called to prophecy bears a similarity to the classic trajectory of becoming a diviner. In some respects, her illness resembles ukuthwasa, with its "persistent symptoms" such as an illness "accompanied by periods of unconsciousness." Diviners typically have dreams and visions in which they receive visitations from ancestors; often they exhibit initial resistance to the call to divination.[24]

The emphasis on regeneration, renewal, and resurrection in Nontetha's transformation is also explicable in terms of Christian beliefs. She stressed her conversion to a new faith. Significantly, the strangers who visited her did not come from the earth, where the ancestors reside, but from the heavens. When they ushered her out of her dwelling, they took her through a new door, which represented Christianity.

Voices revealed that she had a special mission to spread the teachings of the Bible to the uneducated and to preach unity to the chiefs. Perhaps the fact that she was illiterate gave Nontetha an advantage because she could translate Christian beliefs into Xhosa cultural idioms her listeners would readily understand. For instance, the image of the Bible hanging in an umnungumabele tree is particularly evocative. This tree has breast-shaped knobs on it. When a baby resists suckling, the knobs are broken off and the moist part is rubbed on a nursing woman's nipples. While the residue has a sour taste, it induces an infant to suckle. Nontetha's analogy was that since people resist the word of God, the Bible must be made more inviting so the unconverted can receive the word, much like a baby is coaxed to receive the nourishment of mother's milk.[25]

When Nontetha recovered from her illness she thought she had died and been resurrected. But she had to be purified in river water to prepare herself for her new ministry. Her resurrection provides the basis not only for personal renewal, but also for a renewal of her whole society. As a result of the devastating influenza epidemic, her society had undergone a "social death."[26] Nontetha preached that God had punished his people with the illness because he was displeased with them and wanted to convey a clear sign that the end of the world was approaching. However, she offered a way out of their predicament.

Nontetha interpreted the harsh meaning of God's message to people who had succumbed to evil influences. Now they had to change their ways to achieve salvation. Since society had to be purified, she imposed numerous prohibitions and rules on her followers. She strongly opposed tobacco and the heavy consumption of beer (imbara), although beer could be consumed in moderation. She attacked traditional dances, and called for the temporary suspension of circumcision ceremonies. She condemned young men for loitering about and attacked adultery as well as witchcraft. She enjoined her adherents not to eat pork or the meat of any animals that died on their own. "If we realized an animal was sick we had to slaughter it so its blood would be shed."[27] She instructed them not to shake hands with each other as a sign that they were still in mourning.[28]

In the eyes of her followers, her proscriptions erased the distinctions between Christians and non-Christians. Salvation was the immediate goal and previous cleavages were irrelevant. "We did not differentiate between Christians and non-Christians. We were interested in her stressing the importance of a person being saved. And when we joined the movement, she pointed out everything we were doing wrong and we definitely stopped indulging in everything which was not acceptable to her."[29]

Key to Nontetha's message was the day of atonement when Jesus Christ would appear in a cloud to judge both the living and the dead. Christ was described as having fair skin, a beard like grass, and hair like the feathers of a peacock. Although the prophet never predicted an exact day, her followers understood that Judgment Day could happen any time. And when it did, the ancestors who were asleep in their graves would be united with the living.

In her dream she had seen a human face with a beard that encircled jaw and mouth. The face turned into a mountain, Ntaba kaNdoda, a place where the people would be freed of their sins and find salvation.[30] Here she was drawing on a prophecy of the nineteenth-century Xhosa prophet Ntsikana, who told the Xhosa people that when they were liberated they would gather together at Ntaba kaNdoda. This mountain stronghold, which one could see clearly in the distance from Nontetha's home, was a sacred place for Xhosa people, who regarded it reverently as symbolizing Xhosa national unity and as a resting place for heroes of resistance against external invaders.[31]

When Nontetha invoked the image of Ntaba kaNdoda, she was tapping into a long line of Xhosa religious innovators who, responding to the challenge of European intrusion, conquest, and domination of their societies, had crafted messages drawn from Christian and Xhosa symbols and beliefs.

These religious figures represented two prophetic poles. Some nineteenth-century prophets, such as Nxele and Mlanjeni, rejected the European presence and used their prophecies to rouse and mobilize resistance.[32] Nxele, Ntsikana's principal rival, envisioned a world in which Mdalidiphu, the God of the blacks, who was mightier than Thixo, the God of the whites, would drive the European settlers from South Africa. Nxele's message won over Chief Ndlambe, who directed Nxele to lead his soldiers against Europeans in the eastern Cape. When Nxele and his army were routed attacking Grahamstown in 1819, he was imprisoned on Robben Island. The following year he drowned trying to escape. Three decades later Mlanjeni, a teenager renowned for his success at witchcraft eradication, rose to prominence. When the Ndlambe and Ngqika Xhosa went to war against the British in 1850, they relied on Mlanjeni's protective medicines to make the warriors impervious to enemy bullets. However, Mlanjeni's medicines proved ineffectual on the battlefield; he died in disgrace, stricken by tuberculosis in 1853, six months after the war ended.

Another who counseled resistance was the wife of Bhulu, a counselor to the Gqunukwebe chief Kama. Bhulu's wife appeared in Nontetha's area at the same time as the cattle killings in 1856. She prophesied that Kama, who had converted to Christianity in the 1820s, and other African Christians would renounce Christianity and that whites would be "destroyed" because they had killed the son of God. Africans would then be the "favoured race" who would have everything once the whites were "swept from the face of the earth . . . skins, karosses, ornaments, beads will be provided abundantly at Tabendoda."[33]

Although the accounts of these prophets would have been well known to Nontetha, she placed herself at the other end of the spectrum and took her inspiration from a prophet who was Nxele's main rival. His name was Ntsikana and he preached a message of accommodation to Christianity and the expanding European presence. Nontetha explicitly linked herself to Ntsikana by revealing that he had come to her in a dream to tell her that she was the last angel sent from God. Ntsikana instructed her to preach and told her she had a special calling to minister to the chiefs and tell them to pray to God.

A counselor to Chief Ngqika, Ntsikana is recognized as one of the first Xhosa converts to Christianity around 1815. At the time of his death in 1821 his band of followers was quite small, but through his disciples and his hymns, which enjoyed widespread popularity, he had a significant impact on later generations. His major contribution was translating Christian ideas and concepts into terms understandable to a Xhosa audience by using terms rooted in Xhosa culture. As Janet Hodgson has written, Ntsikana's converts "expressed their new beliefs and practices as part of the Xhosa world, living among Xhosa in a Xhosa way."[34]

Ntsikana also anticipated the implications of European expansion and the profound effects it would have on Africans. In one of his visions, he foretold the coming of "people from the west," or European settlers. He warned that change was inescapable and that the Xhosa had to adapt. At the same time he remained wary of European culture and counseled selective borrowing.[35]

In a similar way but in a radically different environment, Nontetha's message blended Xhosa and Christian symbols and employed Xhosa idioms as she accommodated the pervasive influence of Europeans. Her primary audience was the amaqaba. She directed them to become literate and wear European clothes, but she did so within a Xhosa frame of reference.[36]

Ntsikana had sought to purify society by opposing social ills, such as lying, stealing, murder, witchcraft, adultery, fornication, and ritual dances.[37] Under the influence of European mission attitudes toward African culture, succeeding generations of Ntsikana's disciples added *lobola* (bride wealth), polygyny, circumcision, and beer drinking to the list of prohibitions. Like other new converts to Christianity in her area, Nontetha embraced most of these proscriptions, most likely following Ntsikana and his heirs.

Nontetha also saw herself as someone extending the mission of another prominent Xhosa Christian, James Mata Dwane. Before Nontetha began proselytizing, she decided that she had to be baptized. However, she chose to do so not in the Wesleyan Methodist Church, the most prominent church in the area, but in Dwane's Order of Ethiopia.[38] This departure is significant because Dwane himself had lived at the Wesleyan Methodist Annshaw mission station and was an ordained Methodist preacher. Born in 1848 and baptized in 1867, Dwane grew up in the Middledrift area, attended Healdtown Institution, and qualified as a teacher before studying for the ministry. He was ordained in 1881, but he broke with the Wesleyans in 1895 over racism in the church and joined Mangena Mokone's Ethiopian Church, established in 1892. In 1896 the Ethiopian Church sought affiliation with the African-American African Methodist Episcopal (AME) Church. When Dwane took a trip to the

United States in 1896, he was appointed general superintendent of the AME Church in South Africa.

After a series of disputes with the AME Church, he also broke with them and linked himself with the Church of the Province of South Africa. This church had established a semi-autonomous body, the Order of Ethiopia, to accommodate African members and clergy. The Gqunukwebe chief Ngange-lizwe Kama, a Christian, donated land to the order to establish a training college for clergy. But Dwane died in 1916 before he was able to put the college on a firm footing.

In light of Dwane's unfinished task, it is interesting to note that Nontetha specifically articulated her mission as carrying on where Dwane's left off. One of Nontetha's faithful explained: "that those Great Places that Dwane could not reach had to be informed to pray. Dwane was moving about preaching in the Great Places and when he reached eRini [Grahamstown] he became lazy and never approached the *iqaba* but it is stated that the *maqabas* had to pray. Dwane was coming from Debe Nek and went as far as Zigodlo."[39]

Another likely influence on Nontetha's Christianity was through the *umanyano*, the Wesleyan Methodist women's groups that were active in her area. Nontetha's followers later adopted the same name for their group, and there were many other lines of convergence between the two. Methodist umanyanos aimed their proselytizing at women without formal education. They stressed the wearing of uniforms as badges of devotion to the faith, they advocated temperance in the use of alcohol, and they emphasized Bible study and encouraged extemporaneous prayers as well as personal testimonials at services that often stretched through the night.[40]

Nontetha's Prophetic Mission

Even after her vision, Nontetha resisted her calling, pleading that she was just a simple woman and not up to the task. But she was told that if she did not agree to preach, God would send her daughter, Nokazi, in her place. Nontetha reasoned that if it would be difficult for her, it would be even more difficult for her daughter. So reassured by God that he would speak through her, she agreed to begin her mission.

Nontetha initiated her mission by approaching traditional authorities in her area. Her village's headman challenged her by asking whether her husband had given her permission to preach. She responded that her husband's permission did not matter since she had a mission to spread the word of God. She had a similar experience when she approached other chiefs in her area. The most prominent chief was the Gqunukwebe chief Ngangelizwe. When she learned that he was working elsewhere, she established her ministry first among the imiDushane and then among the Ndlambe as far south as East London. According to her followers, some resisted her message, but most recognized the truth she spoke and were contrite and receptive to the word of God. When she returned to Ngangelizwe's place, he consulted his counselors and they allowed her to preach in his area. Her circuit never extended beyond her home area after that.

Nontetha's services normally lasted two to three hours. Prayer services were held in the mornings and evenings. No dancing took place; no drums were used. She taught her disciples hymns that they later learned were Wesleyan Methodist standards, such as the hymns of Ntsikana and *Libadi Labadula* (Like a wandering springbok thirsting for water).[41]

Nontetha usually preached alone, but occasionally one of her devoted assistants led a service. Unable to read, she looked at the palm of her right hand as she preached, as if her message were inscribed there.[42] She often asked her literate believers to read from the Bible. "Read there," she commanded, "and find out if what I say is not there because what I say is not coming from my own mouth but from the Bible." Since she considered herself an instrument of God, her assistants read scripture to reinforce her message and added personal testimonies.

In one of her visions, she had seen a Bible hanging in a tree and had been instructed that although she could not read because she had no schooling, she still had to weave the Bible into her message to the uneducated. The Bible was not for her generation but for generations to come.[43]

Her mission to the uneducated appealed especially to the diviners in her area, and several of them became her leading assistants. One was Gwaru Mshweshwe, identified in a police report as a "native doctor," who said that "God appeared to him and told him to cease Doctoring and take up Nonteto's Religion, to preach to the Red Blanket Natives and convert them."[44]

At her outdoor services, Nontetha wore a white robe and headdress and wrapped a long white sash around her waist. She bore an *umnqayi*, a black stick that senior married women could carry when they attended rituals.[45]

Since many of her supporters were not Christian or Western-educated, they wore traditional clothing. But as the movement gained momentum, she encouraged male converts to wear white coats and shoes purchased from European trading stores. The choice of the color white was significant because of its symbolic importance in Xhosa society. White was associated with the curing of physical abnormalities and other transitions like the ones from boyhood to manhood and the initiation of diviners, who wore white garments. To Xhosa Christians, white also represented goodness, purity, and the "light of Christian-

ity and the gospel."[46] To Nontetha's flock, who wore black
trousers and dresses and white coats and blouses, black represented the destruction God had wrought and white the triumph
of life over death.

At her meetings, her followers sat in front of her in a semi-
circle. Chiefs occupied the front row, counselors the next row,
and adult males the rear. Women stood to one side, while children were placed behind her. As the service began, she would
take off her white sash, lay it on the ground, and kneel on it
because "she was going to ask these people to kneel on the belt
. . . for they were going to ask for unity and their hearts had to
be as white as the belt."[47]

Umanyano, or unity, was a watchword for Nontetha. Her
followers had to respect and remain loyal to the chiefs, but they
also were supposed to strive for solidarity with all Africans.
While she declared she had no intention of subverting chiefly
power, she did criticize their disunity at critical times in the
past. This, she claimed, had brought them to their present
plight. "She . . . said that the Xhosa are divided into various
groups; that had to come to an end. A person should not respect just his own chief. They had to be united."[48]

Umanyano could be achieved only if the chiefs and their
people accepted Christianity. The sins of the present generation
were derived in part from the previous resistance of Africans to
Christian missionaries. "The people had not followed the Bible
faithfully with the advent of the European churches. If they
had, they could have been unified. That they had not followed
the Bible was shown in that they were not unified."[49]

Nontetha's emphasis on the unity of all African peoples did
not, however, imply that she was antiwhite. She asked her followers not to distinguish between blacks and whites and she
called upon the chiefs to pray for the unity of all peoples in the
world.

At first she instructed those of her followers who belonged

to mission churches to remain in them. But as her movement gained strength, she began attacking mission churches—and they in turn attacked her—and forbade her adherents from associating with them. A farmer from the Middledrift area, Pearce Kaba, who attended one of her meetings, remembered: "she condemned the existing churches as the money concerns and being carried on by the white men, as her preachings are that the natives should continue and arrange their own matters without the interference of the white men."[50]

After her meetings, goats were slaughtered as an expression of thanksgiving and to feed those in attendance. One skeptical white concluded, "this naturally appealed to a large number of natives who attended the meetings knowing they would be well fed." But other whites, raising the specter of another cattle-killing episode, were alarmed by the ritual slaughtering. They remembered the catastrophe wrought by the visions of the teenager Nongqawuse, who claimed that she had been visited by the ancestors in April 1856. They instructed her to spread the message that if people slaughtered their cattle and destroyed their granaries, they would be reunited with the ancestors and a golden age would ensue in which Europeans would be expelled from South Africa. The Gcaleka Xhosa king Sarhili, after accepting her prophecy, instructed his people to follow Nongqawuse's injunctions. The results were disastrous to all who participated in the cattle killing. Many thousands of people died of starvation or were left destitute and forced to seek work in European areas.

Whites invoking the memory of the cattle killing drew an immediate response from Nontetha's followers, who did not share their alarmist view that she was sowing the seeds of another cattle killing. "Nongqawuse was telling people about what they were going to gain materially—like God was going to make their granaries full—but Nontetha never said such things. She never made any promises."[51]

2

Bulhoek, Official Memory, and Nontetha

And the fifth angel blew his trumpet, and I saw a star that had fallen on the earth from heaven, to whom was given the key to the pit of the abyss.

He opened the pit of the abyss, and smoke whirled upward from the pit like the smoke of a gigantic furnace, so that the sun and the air were darkened by the smoke of the pit.

Out of the smoke locusts went forth on the earth, such power was granted them as the earth's scorpions possess.

They were not told to damage the earth's grass, neither any tree, but only the persons who do not have the seal of God on their foreheads.

Power was granted them, not to kill them but for five months to torture them, and their torture was like that of a scorpion that stings a person.

During those days people will seek death without finding it; they will be anxious to die, but death evades them.
—Revelation 9:1–6

Nontetha first came to the attention of government officials in mid-1922, when she began holding services in the rural locations near East London. Although some commented positively on her preaching against liquor and her calls for black unity, others were alarmed by reports that she was antiwhite. The Superintendent of Natives at Newlands, Fort Jackson, branded

Nontetha "an undesirable as her theme is chiefly against the white man."[1] In late 1922 additional reports began circulating that she was ordering her adherents not to work on the land or on the mines. Other sources reported that farmworkers in the neighboring districts of Albany and Fort Beaufort were enraptured by her message and were reluctant to return to work.[2]

No matter how alarmist the reports about Nontetha, government officials did not operate with a single mindset toward her. Opinion was divided within the different branches of the state—the South African Police, the Native Affairs Department, the Justice Department, and local magistrates—about the appropriate means of dealing with her. These differences reflected skirmishing that was taking place about the best way to control African protest—whether to deal deftly and sensitively with dissent or take a hard line and suppress it.

Given her efforts to convert "red" people and her preaching against ceremonial beer feasts, witchcraft, and circumcision, some officials considered Nontetha as a conservative rather than a subversive influence. Significantly, Clement Gladwin, who had dealt with Enoch Mgijima's Israelites during the First World War as Kamastone's Superintendent of Natives and who had taken up the same position at Middledrift, argued that the best policy was not to interfere with Nontetha and her followers but to let her movement lose momentum on its own accord. After making a fact-finding visit to Ngcabasa location, he noted the beneficial aspects of Nontetha's message.

> There is a strong feeling of gratitude that the word of God has reached the red natives and similarly that so many are taking up the wearing of European clothing. It is hoped that the converts will later on cleave to the old established denominations and so assist them. Nonteta compares the European successes with the native failures and alleges that the reason is because the latter

have lost their respect for their chiefs and their want of unanimity. Our interpretation of this is that Europeans all worship one God, whereas the natives are divided into Christians and heathens.[3]

However, the memory of the Bulhoek massacre of May 1921 was still vividly etched in the minds of government officials, who were anxious to nip Nontetha's movement in the bud before it escalated into a greater threat.[4] In 1919, Enoch Mgijima, the prophet of an independent church group called the Israelites, had warned his believers of an impending millennium and had instructed them to congregate at his holy village, Ntabelanga at Kamastone, about 100 miles north of Nontetha's area, to await the end of the world. The Israelites informed local government officials that they were gathering to observe their annual Passover festival. But when it became obvious that more Israelites were arriving and staying on without any intention of leaving, the officials were in a quandary about how to deal with the situation. Because they did not have the manpower to enforce the law against the disciplined, uncompromising defiance of the Israelites, they called on Pretoria to intervene.

At various governmental levels, officials employed a variety of tactics to pressure the Israelites to leave Ntabelanga—issuing summonses to evict squatters, sending a small police force in December 1920 to intimidate the Israelites, and making three attempts at negotiating a settlement. First the government sent out a delegation of government officials, then a group of moderate Africans, and finally the newly established Native Affairs Commission. But none of these attempts succeeded. The government concluded that the Israelites had to be evicted by force, and a police unit of 800 men drawn from all over South Africa was ordered to go to Bulhoek for a showdown. On 24 May 1921 the police, armed with rifles and machine guns, clashed with the Israelites, bearing only assegais and knobkerries. Nearly 200 Israelites died in the battle.

The Bulhoek massacre left an indelible imprint on official attitudes toward prophetic movements. That is why despite the fact that some officials recognized the redeeming features of Nontetha's movement, the perception of an antiwhite message on her part set off alarms and convinced factions in the government that if she were not removed from the scene, her movement could mushroom into even more of a menace. No official wanted to be scapegoated if Nontetha and her followers proved to be an embarrassment to the government.

This apprehension on the part of many white officials, especially the police, grew into such a consuming security psychosis that sounding the tocsin of Bulhoek was all that was needed to override other considerations. A white trader, Sidney Jakins, warned, "It was quite evident that the movement has the religious aspect merely as a blind and that this aim was for the down fall of the Europeans. I am confident that if these movements had not been stopped [they] would have led to serious trouble, probably bloodshed similar to the Bullhoek affair."[5]

Writing about Nontetha and her adherents, the Superintendent of Natives at Berlin stated: "As their persuasion is identical with that of the Israelites, which ended so drastically at Bull Hoek."[6] A King William's Town official put it: "In view of the Bullhoek developments the subsequent steps of the movement here can be readily visualised." And a report emanating from Pretoria similarly concluded: "The religious aspects of Nonteta's activities are regarded as cloaking a more serious objective, for information has been received that her followers discuss the overthrowing of the Europeans by a combination of the black races and the coming of the American Negroes."[7]

In the initial stage of dealing with the Israelites, one option government officials explored was seizing the prophet Mgijima in the hope that, without his charismatic leadership, the movement would lose its bearing and disintegrate. Alert to this possibility, the Israelite leaders had not allowed Mgijima to participate directly in any negotiations with the government. In the case of Nontetha, the government reconsidered this option, apparently calculating that separating her from her followers would not provoke a public outcry.

As it turned out, in this regard they were correct. In the months leading up to the Bulhoek massacre and especially after it, many prominent black leaders and organizations voiced sympathy for the Israelites and opposition to the government's use of brute force to crush them. In contrast, when Nontetha was arrested and jailed in King William's Town in late 1922, no one outside her immediate area came to her defense.

However, Nontetha's arrest did not deter her followers. Braving floodwaters, several hundred of them congregated outside the King William's Town courthouse singing hymns and chanting prayers. But the government was determined not to let Nontetha resume her preaching right away. Nevertheless, she was not tried for any civil offense; instead she was committed to Fort Beaufort Mental Hospital on 6 December 1922 for "medical observation." The hospital released her on 5 January 1923 on six months' probation, on the condition that she refrain from preaching.[8] But her release was not coordinated with the Middledrift magistrate, who was caught by surprise; he instructed hospital officials not to release her again without giving him prior warning.

Nontetha disregarded the condition of her release—that she refrain from preaching. As stories of her continuing "seditious" activities trickled in, officials recommitted her at Fort Beaufort on 7 April 1923 for an indefinite period. According to her followers, Nontetha predicted that this would happen. In fact she specified that she would be arrested twice—the first time for a short period and the second time for a long period. When the authorities came for her at Peuleni location in April 1923 to recommit her, her followers wanted to resist, but she persuaded them not to interfere.[9]

If the authorities expected that Nontetha's movement would lose momentum in her absence, they were sadly mistaken. Her assistants Gwaru Mshweshwe, Kegu Mpendu, Booi Lama, Mama Ntosini, Joni Zana, and Reuben Tsoko carried on her work. Her movement also gained credibility and an added impetus from the participation of the wife of Chief Ngangelizwe Kama, who allowed Nontetha's followers to continue holding meetings at his homestead.

During this period, resident magistrates oversaw administration of the African reserves, but they relied on chiefs and headmen to carry out policy. Consequently, when local officials moved to break up Nontetha's movement, they called upon chiefs and headmen in her area to ban their meetings. The approach was frustrated in one area because Ngangelizwe Kama was off working in the Grahamstown area, and his nephew Tamsanqa Kama was acting in his place. Ngangelizwe had been appointed "acting" chief of the Gqunukwebe on 1 March 1899 when his uncle William Shaw Kama had died childless. Ngangelizwe was not the legitimate claimant to the chieftainship since he was the second son of Samuel Kama, William Shaw's elder brother, who predeceased him. But Samuel's eldest son, Lutili, had also died and Lutili's son, Tamsanqa, was too young to be named chief. Tamsanqa agreed not to challenge his uncle's right to rule as regent during his lifetime in return for a commitment from Ngangelizwe that he name Tamsanqa as his successor. Despite this understanding, an underlying tension clearly existed between the two.[10]

Shortly after Nontetha was recommitted in April 1923, Tamsanqa, supported by Ngangelizwe's counselors and headmen, called Nontetha's followers to his kraal and ordered them to stop their meetings. He reminded them that in the past, their forefathers had been loyal to the government, that they had fought with the Cape government against the Ngqika Xhosa chief Sandile and other African "rebels" in the war of 1850–53, and that they had been rewarded with land grants on the condition that they remained loyal.[11] Warning that the continued meetings of Nontetha's followers jeopardized everyone's welfare, Tamsanqa ordered them to disperse and return to their homes. They agreed, but a few days later, Tamsanqa received reports from his counselors that services were surreptitiously being held late at night.[12]

A police account of a midnight service at Joni Zana's homestead reported:

> Yamile Bele . . . addressed the meeting telling the people to follow the preaching of Nonteta. He was questioned by a man named Sosini who asked him whether they would not get into trouble by continuing these gatherings in view of the fact that the Acting Chief had put a stop to it. He answered "No we won't get into trouble because these gatherings are also held at the kraal of Chief Gangelizwe Kama, our Chief; but that they had only to be careful and continue to keep the gatherings during night so that the Police do not see them gather." At day break this meeting dispersed.[13]

On another occasion Sgt. J. A. Wagenaar heard that one of Nontetha's converts acted out the story of her death and resurrection. After he fell to the ground and pretended to be dead, others placed blankets over him. They "pray and sing round him for a long time when he would rise and pretend that he had risen from the death [*sic*]."[14]

The active encouragement of Chief Ngangelizwe's wife also severely undermined Tamsanqa's authority. Calling together his counselors, Tamsanqa confronted her at Ngangelizwe's kraal: "he asked what right she had to continue these meetings after the chiefs and councillors had stopped it, she answered that she had to be consulted first before a stop could be put to it and even Gangelizwe would have consulted her before he had done such a thing." When Tamsanqa challenged her, "Do you know that I was left by Chief Gangelizwe Kama to act for him during his absence?" she retorted, "Yes I know but you should have first consulted me before you had done anything in the matter." Chief Tamsanqa countered, "According to our native custom, we do not consult women in matters of this nature." Ngangelizwe's wife did not accept Tamsanqa's position on women, and she broke off the exchange, making it clear that the meetings would continue until God stopped them.[15]

In the face of such defiance, Tamsanqa and his counselors decided that the only way to break the impasse was to bring Ngangelizwe back home. However, the messengers sent to find him were unsuccessful, and Tamsanqa had to wait until mid-1923 for his return. Nevertheless, they were convinced that the majority of Kama's people were behind them. Along with white officials they were confident that the movement had lost its momentum and that the trouble would blow over in the near future. However, as in the case of the Bulhoek massacre, there was a major difference between official perception and what was really happening on the ground.

This difference became apparent a few months after Nontetha's recommittal in April, when her assistants set out to win more converts. Among her most enthusiastic supporters were children who dropped out of schools to follow her. Elliott Gara, who taught in a location that was a Nontetha stronghold, reported in August 1923 that of the 110 children enrolled in his school the previous quarter, only fifty were still in attendance.[16]

Although Nontetha was confined in a place fifty miles away, her disciples streamed back and forth between their homes and the hospital to seek her guidance. The assumption that Nontetha's movement would die out if she herself were out of the picture vastly underestimated the tremendous loyalty and dedication of her supporters.

A Plague of Locusts

According to her followers, Nontetha, before she was arrested, had predicted that an invasion of locusts would sweep through the region.[17] She proclaimed God had sent them as a punishment and decreed that none be killed. When a swarm of *voetganger* locusts descended on the area in September and October 1923, government officials ordered the people to kill them, invoking the Agricultural Pest Act of 1911, which empowered the government to order any citizen to kill insects.

When Nontetha's followers refused to kill the locusts, officials had a legal pretext for disrupting the movement. As one police officer commented: "As far as I can gather the local Chief and Headman are strongly against the movement and are doing their best to discourage it, but having no means of authority beyond moral persuasion they are handicapped, and because there is no infringement of any law, the followers of Nonteta feel they can do as they like with impunity. Their refusal to obey a lawful order of Court was however a serious matter and was bound to have serious consequence hence my determination to check it at once."[18]

J. W. Ord, Clement Gladwin's successor as acting magistrate of Middledrift, believed the sect was an offshoot of the Israelites. He described one encounter with Nontetha's followers when he tried to enforce the locust killing:

As we approached about 40 of them threw themselves on the ground and commenced praying and singing. At first they declined to take any notice of my requests but after separating the women (who were the most virulent) the Headmen requested the men to proceed to destroy locusts which were in enormous swarms around the kraals. This they all declined to do in a most emphatic manner. I thereafter noticed 5 men in white suits led by one also wearing a red handkerchief—going through very weird physical contortions. The five seemed quite irresponsible and unable to control their behaviour. Their actions were those of a man who had taken poison. I ordered that they should be sent into King Williamstown for medical examination and observation.[19]

On 22 October 1923 the policemen sent out to Ngcabasa location arrested seven male members of the sect for refusing to kill locusts. They were ordered to pay fines of £3 or serve ten-day sentences. When police descended on the location a week later, they went to several places where Nontetha's followers had congregated and directed them to cooperate in killing locusts. At one meeting place the followers formed a tight circle three or four people deep. When Constable J. N. Daas tried to serve a summons on any of them, "they would all kneel down and pray and shout at the top of their voices. Those upon whom I served summons would not listen and immediately either tore up or threw away the summons. Upon my endeavouring to enter the ring to serve the summonses they all bunched together and by weight of numbers forced me out. They did not use their hands, however, only pushed me out with the weight of their bodies."[20]

On 12 November policemen, this time accompanied by Ngangelizwe Kama, his counselors, and the Ngcabasa headman, raided the movement's meeting places in Ngcabasa. One hundred thirty-five people were arrested, but no physical clashes ensued because Nontetha's followers passively resisted by "throwing themselves on the ground singing and praying." Although chiefs and headmen attempted to persuade them to go along peacefully, the police had to push their prisoners, with "other natives hanging on to the persons of those being arrested by the Police." The prisoners were marched first to nearby Fort White and then to Middledrift and King William's Town, where they had to await trial. They were sentenced to pay fines varying from one to five pounds or to serve one- to two-week jail sentences with hard labor. All of them chose the latter.[21]

While Nontetha's followers were in jail, they conducted services, prayed, and sang. Some had dreams about African-Americans liberating South Africa. Rumors of African-American liberators had spread throughout South Africa after the First World War, largely due to the expectations of change roused by disciples of Marcus Garvey's Universal Negro Improvement Association. In discussions of African unity among Nontetha's followers, the names of Garvey and Clements Kadalie, leader of the Industrial and Commercial Workers' Union, frequently cropped up.[22] When the dreams of liberation were discussed, some interpreted them to mean that African-Americans would come, unlock the doors of their jail cells, and set them free. "We used to dream in the hope that the Americans were coming to release us. It was just a rumor, but what you hear as a rumor, you always dream about. I can't tell you who told us these rumors but there was always hope throughout that the Americans would free us. As oppressed people, we always had hope that we would be released."[23] To others, the dreams roused unrealistic hopes and led to disillusionment. One such follower who quit the movement mused afterward: "Liars stated that they had dreamt seeing the Americans opening the doors of the jail. When I awoke I didn't see the Americans; all I saw was the police."[24]

The fascination of Nontetha's supporters with African-American liberators did not end with the jail dreams. A Zulu Garveyite disciple who claimed to be a black American, "Dr." Wellington Buthelezi, had electrified many parts of the Transkei in the 1920s with his predictions of African-American liberators who would free South Africa from white oppression. When Buthelezi visited Nontetha at Weskoppies Hospital in Pretoria, where she had been transferred, he won her favor.

Although Buthelezi visited their area several times and held meetings, the alliance was fleeting and Nontetha's flock eventually formed their own church, the Church of the Prophetess Nontetha.[25] However, in the coming decades, the American influence lingered on. Nontetha's followers never forgot her advice, "Look to the Americans. They will help you one day." And, in an unexpected way, her words were fulfilled in the last years of the century.

When Nontetha's followers had served their jail time, they returned to their homes. But again they refused to kill locusts, and additional sentences were imposed on many of them. The jail terms dampened the fervor of some, who concluded that further participation in the movement was bound to lead to more confrontations with the government. A former follower expressed his disillusionment this way: "I thought I was going to heaven, but I went to jail instead."[26] Others who had converted to Christianity because of Nontetha found that, in her absence, her movement did not satisfy many of their pressing questions about Christianity, such as baptism and the Sabbath.[27] Some joined mission churches, while others were attracted to independent churches, such as James Limba's Bantu Church of Christ.[28]

Portrait of Nontetha, painted by Lizo Pemba

Taba kaNdoda (Mount Ndoda) *(Cory Library, Rhodes University)*

Fort Cox *(Cory Library, Rhodes University)*

A MAD PROPHETESS.

D.D. Jan. 14. 1927

Followers Trek to Pretoria.

PRETORIA, Thursday. (Reuter).—About eighteen women and eighteen men arrived in Pretoria yesterday from the Cape, whence they started out on foot on November 23 for the purpose of visiting Nonteta, the Israelite prophetess, a Xosa woman at present an inmate of the Mental Hospital. Some years ago she was the leader of a native movement in the Cape, near King Williamstown. This movement resembled in many respects the Israelite movement which resulted in the Bullhoek affair. Nonteta was found to be mentally deranged, and was removed to the Mental Hospital at the capital. Her following number several hundreds at the Cape, and her thirty-six visitors have trekked up to the Transvaal with the avowed intent of obtaining her release from the Mental Hospital, but it is not expected that their hopes will be realised.

The movement of which Nonteta is the leader is not approved of by the Government on account of its politics. It is opposed to the white races, but in some other respects their tenets are fairly sound. They are definitely opposed to the sale of Kaffir beer, and have strong temperance convictions, but the church comes under the ban of their disapproval, their view being that that body is a money-making concern. On political grounds their teaching is entirely against the Government and, indeed, to any form of progress. They predict that the Day of Judgment may be expected at any time.

"PROPHETESS" AMONG PHILISTINES

NATIVE FOLLOWER'S PASSIVE RESISTANCE

To rescue Nonteta, their prophetess, from the hands of the "Philistines," her followers have shown that they are prepared to endure insults, hardships and tribulation, and are now busy in demonstrating to the authorities in Pretoria the extent to which they are prepared to sacrifice personal comfort and convenience for the sake of what is to them an ideal.

Nonteta, as already reported in the "Rand Daily Mail," is in the Pretoria Mental Asylum, and recently 36 of her followers arrived from Kingwilliamstown, having walked all the way, to try to secure her release.

The authorities have proved adamant, and the latest development in this curious battle is the adoption of passive resistance tactics by Nonteta's followers. They definitely refuse to leave Pretoria until Nonteta is released.

As a result, twelve were arrested and charged under the pass-laws on Monday, being fined £1 each, the sentence to be suspended for 24 hours on condition that they left Pretoria. Late yesterday afternoon the period of suspension terminated, but they were still in Pretoria.

They will now be arrested, and will probably be charged under the Urban Areas Act.

Newspaper articles from the East London *Daily Dispatch* and the *Rand Daily Mail* covering the 1927 "Pilgrimage of Grace"

Outdoor eating shed at Tower Mental Hospital, Fort Beaufort
(Hilary Sapire)

Building of Tower Mental Hospital (now used as a high school)
(Hilary Sapire)

Weskoppies Mental Hospital, c. 1908 *(Weskoppies Mental Hospital)*

Dr. J. T. Dunston, Physician
Superintendent of Weskop-
pies Hospital, 1922 *(Weskoppies Mental Hospital)*

Conference of Physician Superintendents of Mental Hospitals,
1923. Dr. J. T. Dunston is second to the left on the bottom row;
Dr. F. D. Crosthwaite is second to the right on the top row.
(Weskoppies Mental Hospital)

Patient at Weskoppies Mental Hospital, 1937 *(Ralph J. Bunche Collection, University of California at Los Angeles)*

Patients at Weskoppies Mental Hospital, 1937 *(Ralph J. Bunche Collection, University of California at Los Angeles)*

3

Of Unsound Mind

John remarked to me: "The Christian religion muddles
some native brains. I hear so much silly talk when these
people think they are God, Jesus Christ or Satan . . ."
—Wulf Sachs, *Black Hamlet*

Most government officials who had dealt with Nontetha's
movement welcomed her sequestration as a way to remove
her on a more-or-less permanent basis and thus to avert a repetition of the Bulhoek debacle. Moreover, by "pathologizing" a
seeming act of subversion, the authorities believed that they
could strip Nontetha's movement of any legitimacy. Having
finally disposed of Nontetha in Fort Beaufort Mental Hospital, a relieved magistrate expressed this attitude in December
1922. "The fact that its priestess has been declared insane," he
said, "will do much to extinguish the faith of the Red adherents."[1]

Such was not the case, however. On the contrary, Nontetha's
incarceration infused the movement with fresh urgency and a
renewed sense of mission. Neither followers and family nor
sympathizers ever accepted the medical rationale, with its implied humanitarian motivation, for her confinement. They con-
tinually challenged the allegation of mental disturbance and
the legitimacy of her confinement throughout the long years
of campaigning for Nontetha's release. In the eyes of her fol-

lowers and supporters, keeping Nontetha in a mental hospital was no different from locking her up in a jail. Given the predominantly custodial functions of mental hospitals, particularly for black patients, as well as the specific circumstances of Nontetha's incarceration, this view had an irrefutable cogency.

Although political questions of power and domination lay at the heart of this conflict between Nontetha's followers, state officials, and representatives of the psychiatric profession about her state of mind, this dialogue also reveals a fundamental tension between African and Western attitudes toward mental illnesses and their treatments. This conflict occurred against a background of the consolidation of psychiatry as a medical specialization in South Africa, as well as an accompanying surge in the numbers of Africans confined in South African mental hospitals. These developments were coupled with the emergence of increasingly racialized psychiatric discourses and practices that, as several scholars have shown, both dovetailed with, and served the purposes of racial segregation and the maintenance of white supremacy.[2]

Troublesome Persons

In passing through the maze of courts and jails in the Cape's criminal justice system only to end up in mental hospitals, Nontetha traversed the same path to institutionalization as had the majority of Africans labeled mentally ill during the late nineteenth and early twentieth centuries. As in most of colonial Africa, Africans only rarely brought their mentally disturbed kin directly to the asylums voluntarily. The colonial authorities, moreover, invariably only confined deranged Africans in asylums when they disrupted the regimes and disciplines of work on white farms, in the kitchens, and mines or when they threatened social peace more generally, whether in the streets or "native reserves." The primary concern in confining mad Africans thus was less with "curing" or alleviating their mental pain than with removing them as a source of disturbance to society at large.

In the early to mid-nineteenth century, whereas the jails were used to accommodate the most dangerous "lunatics," the old Somerset Hospital in Cape Town and the asylum on Robben Island were the only public medical institutions that accommodated the mentally disordered of all colors and ethnic designations. By the latter years of the century, in the wake of South Africa's industrial revolution, however, a network of asylums sprang up at the Cape, Natal, Orange Free State, and Transvaal. Legislative amendments in 1879 and 1891 to the lunacy ordinances of the 1830s provided ever more precise distinctions between the "dangerously insane," "criminal lunatics," and persons "of unsound mind." From 1891, magistrates, and not only the governor, were empowered to commit "ordinary lunatics" to asylums. As a consequence of these legislative and institutional changes, those individuals defined as insane found themselves confined in state-supported asylum systems, which quarantined them physically and symbolically from the larger society, with their condition diagnosed as a uniquely and essentially medical problem.[3]

Asylums thus offered a means of removing troublesome and dangerous lunatics—white and black—from society, but within a humanitarian and medical framework that differentiated their confinements from those of mere criminals. Directly, in the case of the two British colonies—the Cape and Natal—and indirectly in the case of the Transvaal and Orange Free State republics, this occurred under the auspices of the British as British-styled institutions were diffused throughout the empire.

Andrew Scull has argued that the emergence of the asylum in nineteenth-century Britain was associated with the transition from the old paternalistic social order to a modern commercial consumer society. The changed perceptions that marked this transition, he contends, heightened the politically dominant bourgeoisie's dissatisfaction with traditional non-institutional responses to the indigent. Increasingly, institutionally based systems of workhouses and asylums became attractive as they were seen to guarantee an efficient and economic solution to the problem, a close and continuing watch on inmates, and the best means of establishing proper work habits among those most resistant to industrialized labor. In this process, attitudes toward the deranged changed decisively. They were now to be differentiated from a wider category of the merely indigent and troublesome. Mental illness shifted from a vague, culturally defined phenomenon into a condition that could be authoritatively diagnosed, certified, and treated by a group of legally recognized experts. Asylums were endorsed as the sole officially approved response to mental illness, and alienists (asylum doctors) constituted themselves as a newly self-conscious profession, based on control over the new realm of asylumdom.[4]

Although similar institutions were transplanted in colonial South Africa as a fact of British imperialism, analogous internal pressures associated with the expansion of a "robust and abrasive commercialism" and the desire of the newly established responsible government at the Cape (1872) to regulate social deviancy more effectively were critical to the expansion of the asylum system in the Cape from the mid-nineteenth century. From early on, however, a clearly differentiated system of mental health provision on the basis of race as well as class emerged. Whereas the Grahamstown and Valkenberg asylums offered humanitarian and enlightened care for mostly middle-class or white patients, Port Alfred catered to chronic cases, and served as a custodial institution for removing troublesome, disruptive, and violent Africans from society.[5]

If mental health provision was profoundly racialized (and gendered) from its inception, the asylums also shared many characteristics with those of prisons. The tie between prisons and asylums was, and long remained, an intimate one. Some of the most ardent calls for the establishment of asylums in late-nineteenth-century South Africa came from the prisons, where the deranged and distracted had been routinely confined, and whose disruptive and unsettling presence had come to jeopardize the maintenance of penal discipline and order. Significantly, even after the establishment of asylums, the close association with the penal system remained, both in the custodial image of the asylum and in institutional arrangements. For no sooner were asylums established than they became rapidly overcrowded, leaving little other option to the authorities than to continue confining the insane in jails. In 1911 as many as 781 mentally disturbed individuals were accommodated in South Africa's prisons, a figure considered scandalous by the authorities.[6] Even in periods of asylum expansion, which (temporarily) alleviated space shortages, for many African inmates a spell in jail represented a way station to incarceration in a mental hospital.[7] As urbanization gathered pace in the twentieth century, more and more Africans entered the criminal justice and penal systems, often as a consequence of minor infractions, such as failure to present a pass or violation of location regulations and curfews. The notoriously brutal conditions of South Africa's prisons undoubtedly played their part in unsettling and disturbing inmates, some of whom showed signs of becoming mentally disordered only after their incarceration. As one African visitor to Pretoria Mental Hospital noted in the late 1930s, many of the African inmates "came to the asylum from prison." "How cruel the white people are!" he went on, "If these men had committed murder, why didn't they hang them? Why torture them, make them mad?"[8]

Within the Cape itself, there were also distinctive regional pressures. In the eastern Cape, where Nontetha lived and preached, the growth of asylums was intimately associated with the violence of frontier society. Asylums grew up in the wake of the protracted struggle for dominance between white and black and the fragmentation of African societies that followed conquest, settler expansion, and the exodus of African men to the labor markets of the Cape and elsewhere. Settler and official concerns about ensuring stable and prosperous European communities in this historic zone of conflict, with its numerically dominant African population, and about maintaining social order directly imprinted themselves on the institutional cultures and practices of asylums.

As an African woman, Nontetha was statistically less likely than either African men or whites of either gender to end up in a mental hospital. Whereas minimal provision was initially made for black inmates of asylums, their numbers, particularly of men, grew markedly with the increasing incorporation of African societies into the colonial social order and labor market by the late nineteenth century. Farm laborers, domestic servants, and urban workers whose crazed behaviors rendered them a danger to social peace were "arrested by the police, taken to gaol, and from there harried on to the Asylum." White farmers in the eastern Cape gratefully turned to the asylums as a means of removing "troublesome insane [African] persons" from their properties.[9] An explanation for the larger proportion of African men than African women being incarcerated in asylums may lie in their greater proximity to European worlds through migrant labor, and thus the higher visibility to Europeans of aberrant behaviors.[10] However, the many social strains experienced within African reserve societies following

conquest, land dispossession, and successive disease and envi-
ronmental disasters in the closing decades of the nineteenth
century undoubtedly also contributed to the growth in numbers of men and women African inmates in asylums. Those
who were neither amenable to care or who constituted an un-
wanted burden on fragile kinship networks increasingly found
themselves committed to one or other of the asylums from the
late nineteenth century. Thus Babase Magame, the elderly
daughter of a Ngqika chief, who had been "wandering in her
head" for seven years, keeping body and soul together by beg-
ging and stealing, was removed from the location in Grahamstown to the Grahamstown asylum and thence as a chronic case
to the Fort Beaufort asylum in 1895.[11]

A fuller explanation for the differential rate at which men
and women were incorporated into the asylum system, especially in these early years, thus needs to go further than noting the demographic effects of migrant labor. It is likely, as
discussed later in this chapter, that women's relatively more
significant participation in a range of healing, spirit-posses-
sion cults, and prayer networks offered psychological outlets
and means of negotiating the strains of a rapidly changing
way of life. When those and other safety nets failed them, it
was as destitutes and vagrants that African women commonly
came to the attention of the white authorities. Liza Mglamine
was one such individual who was brought before the Middelburg magistrates' court on charges of vagrancy in 1928. The
court determined that she was "not mentally sound," sent her
to the Fort Beaufort asylum, and sought to find refuge for her
two young children with the Lourdes Mission in Griqualand
East.[12]

Moreover, a powerfully racialized and gendered psychiatric
discourse and attitudes determined different responses by psychiatrists to presentations of African madness, with African
males more likely to be stigmatized as dangerous and thus re-

quiring sequestration. Indeed, the Secretary of Native Affairs was moved to suggest in 1909 that the pass documents of African men discharged from asylums should include the information that they had been incarcerated in such institutions. "You or I or anybody else might innocently engage such a native and expose our families to the utmost danger," he warned.[13]

By the late nineteenth century, argues Harriet Deacon, the earlier unsystematized social and racial prejudices that had informed medical practices in asylums were replaced by an explicitly theorized, pseudoscientific colonial psychiatry that increasingly justified the need for separate and different treatment for white and black.[14] These theories, in turn, were an outgrowth of late Victorian and early Edwardian anxieties regarding the "nervous degeneration" of the European races and the dangerous possibility of their regressing into "savage" states, particularly on the colonial fringes, where the maintenance of social and sexual boundaries between colonizer and colonized was considered paramount to the preservation of white supremacy. This was reflected in the more effective "policing" of white conduct and deviance—including intemperance, juvenile delinquency, transgressing sexual and racial taboos—in which psychiatry increasingly had a role to play.[15]

By the early twentieth century, concerns about white racial health by white professionals, scientists, and popular writers were complemented by a growing fascination with "the native mind," involving such questions as whether African brain structures were different from those of whites, attempts to determine the distinctive character of "native mentality," investigations into the place of witchcraft and African cosmology, and whether Africans' intelligence could reliably be measured and compared with that of whites.[16] Psychiatrists working in South Africa's asylums both drew upon, and contributed to this growing body of "knowledge" about "African mentality," particularly in their theories about the irremediably different ways in which African and Europeans went mad.

One theory, favored by Thomas Duncan Greenlees, superintendent of the Grahamstown asylum, was that it was "civilization" itself that had unhinged the African mind. The asylum was receiving ever greater numbers of African men "who from the civilising influences of their surroundings seem readily to break down mentally." These men were to be distinguished from those leading "a simple and savage existence" in the reserves, rhapsodized Greenlees, "a life in the open air, in a perfect climate, with plenty of simple and natural food."[17] In a similar vein, a medical officer of Pretoria Mental Hospital observed in 1910 that "practically all our recurrent and returned cases amongst natives are due to one of two things, namely: dagga [marijuana] smoking or alcohol," and that repatriation of all discharged "native lunatics" to their "kraals" was desirable.[18]

Such ideas about the savage simplicity of reserve life went hand in hand with assumptions that Africans suffered simpler forms of insanity than those of Europeans. By virtue of the latter's higher mental development, their insanity was considerably more complex and difficult to cure. These idealized notions of the healthy conditions in the reserves as well as ideas about Africans' capacity to recover sooner from insanity than whites persisted well into the twentieth century. They dovetailed with segregationist ideas of the 1910s, 1920s, and 1930s that Africans were "naturally" part of the land and that the cities were a corrosive source of decay and pollution from which Africans should be shielded.[19] They also justified minimal state provision of mental health facilities for Africans and their rapid repatriation from mental asylums. As the Secretary for Native Affairs commented in February 1910, repatriation would ensure that "the patients may have a complete rest at their own kraals to strengthen their recovery."[20]

Although psychiatrists in the asylums sought to keep African numbers in the institutions to the minimum, to dispatch manageable cases to the "kraals," and to restrict long-term inmates to "the more violent cases,"[21] this did not imply that they did not believe that mental illness occurred among Africans in "traditional" society. Too many cases of inexplicable hut burnings, random acts of violence, assaults on children, and other aberrant behaviors in the reserves and on farms came to their attention.

Moreover, some writers went so far as to brand aspects of "normal" African life, such as witchcraft beliefs or "ancestor worship," as pathological. In 1910 the superintendent of the Fort Beaufort asylum, Dr. J. Conry, identified "native customs" like circumcision as among the causes of insanity among Africans.[22] Nearly twenty years later, Dr. B. J. F. Laubscher, the superintendent of Komani Mental Hospital in Queenstown, argued that *ukuthwasa* represented psychoneurotic symptoms (delusions and hallucinations) that Africans simply were unable to identify. For Laubscher, this failure proved the irredeemably irrational, myth-soaked nature of Tembu culture.[23] In similarly essentialist vein, a contemporary, A. T. Bryant, commented, "[T]he Africans being a race of strong emotions, both sexually and sentimentally, we should almost expect hysteria to be rife among them."[24]

In addition, although reserves were portrayed as sanatoria for the demented, writers were as likely to look with disdain upon African practitioners and healers, such as *inyangas* (dispensers of herbal medicines) who treated them. Moreover, legislative interventions such as Medical, Dental and Pharmacy Act no. 13 of 1928 actively sought to curb their activities. This act prevented African herbalists and "native medicine men" from practicing outside Natal. At its most extreme, as one inyanga observed, "white people often sent sangomas [diviners] to the asylum because they think them mad." Indeed,

as the psychiatrist Dr. Laubscher observed, many African healers and diviners "conform broadly to the class of abnormal
characters known in our culture as psychopaths."[25]

As this brief survey can only begin to indicate, official attitudes toward the treatment of the African insane were shot
through with contradictions throughout the period of Nontetha's incarceration. On the one hand, there was a huge gulf
between theory and practice. A great deal of energy was ex-
pended in exploring the contours of "the native mind" and the
depths of "the native personality." Theories ranged from those
that emphasized the "normally pathological" nature of African
cultures to those that made claims for highly sexualized, emotionally volatile tendencies inherent in the African personality. On the other hand, in institutional terms, the relevant state
departments and psychiatrists were anxious to restrict the
African presence in the asylums to those who were seen to
constitute a danger to society at large, and (to a lesser extent)
themselves. As far as possible, they sought to dispatch the insane to the rural reserves and farms, where their kin and communities were expected to care for them. Although the limited
resources and facilities at the disposal of state psychiatric institutions were a powerful incentive to exclude Africans as far
as possible, both this policy, as well as differential treatment of
black and white within asylums, were justified by a discourse
that portrayed African forms of insanity as relatively simple
and the reserves as appropriately recuperative environments.
This meant that apart from the limited care that mission hospitals were able to extend, Africans were largely excluded from
whatever therapeutic benefits the psychiatric profession had
to offer. At the same time, "traditional" treatments of the mentally disordered (and indeed, those afflicted by other forms
of illness) by inyangas and sangomas were looked upon with
hostility by the medical establishment and constrained by legislation.

African Conceptions of Madness

Despite profound differences in diagnoses, causal explanations, and desired treatments, areas of agreement could exist between Africans and white psychiatrists about the fact of a person behaving in an aberrant fashion. Both parties, for example, could agree that persons who randomly set fire to their homes or physically attacked others for no apparent reason were disturbed. In Nontetha's case, however, there was agreement neither about her state of mind nor about how she should be treated. Whereas the authorities and psychiatrists came to regard Nontetha as insane and to treat her accordingly, none of the Africans whose lives she touched, whether they were her followers or those who became acquainted with her story, ever referred to her behavior as *ubugeza*. *Ubugeza* is the Xhosa word for madness. It encompasses extreme folly, headstrong passion, and rashness that express themselves in irrational acts, fury, or rage, and it probably comes closest to the psychiatrists' descriptions of Nontetha's actions and behaviors at Fort Beaufort and Weskoppies Mental Hospitals. Nor was she described by the Xhosa words for other forms of derangement—*ukubuda*, *ubuhlanya*, and *izezo zobugeza*—nor the words and phrases describing dysphoric states, such as *matshekile, khathazekile,* or *intliziyo ibuhlungu* (the heart is painful).[26] Even those Africans who had been hostile to Nontetha's preaching and who had provided eyewitness statements to the police prior to her arrest portrayed her as subversive and difficult, rather than as mad.

However, as the very existence of a lexicon of madness indicates, although Nontetha was not considered to be insane, hers and other African societies indeed did identify a range of mental afflictions that manifested themselves in frenzied, violent, and irrational acts, in dysphoric, melancholic states, as well as in the "loss of senses" which included stupors and fits. As with afflictions that displayed themselves in somatic or physiological symptoms, there was a range of healing methods to treat these affective or behavioral disorders. A. T. Bryant, for example, writes of *amaHabiya*, which was made up of animal fats or the roots of the *uKhathwa* herb, the *umMbehezi* tree, or the *amaPhofu* bush to combat the charms made up of the same substances, used by young men to induce "hysteria" in young women in Zulu societies. Temporary insanity or delirium— *uHlanyana*—could be treated by the poisonous bulb of the forest climber *inGcolo* boiled in water.[27] Conditions that some writers categorize as "African cultural diseases" *(ukufa kwabantu)*, including spirit possession, sorcery, poisoning, and pollution, were similarly all amenable to treatment by healers and healer-prophets, with recourse to Western psychiatry representing only one of a range of therapeutic options—usually the last choice.[28]

In *Black Hamlet*, Wulf Sachs recounts the way in which the Manyika nyanga John Chawafambira diagnosed the deranged and violent behavior of his mother-in-law, Mawa, as a consequence of poisoning at the hands of a malevolent relative, a witch. His task as healer was to discover how the poison had entered Mawa's body, to treat her by appealing to the *miszumu* (spirit of the ancestors), and to apply protective medicines and various rituals. Only as a last resort, when his own methods failed, did John appeal to the European doctor Wulf Sachs to administer the latter's medicine. It was also only after Mawa was convicted for the murder of her four-year-old daughter that she was delivered into the hands of Western psychiatrists in a mental hospital.[29]

Despite differences within them, notably between Nguni and Sotho-Tswana, a major contrast between African healing cultures, with their emphasis on collective, social responses to afflictions and those of Western psychiatry was the absence in the former, of traditions of separating the deranged and disruptive from their communities. "To segregate a man from society was unknown," observed the Rev. Henri Phillipe Junod of Tsonga society. Only in the most extreme instances, when dangerous madness has seized a person, was physical restraint and forcible restraint adopted:

> and he or she was put into the stocks called by Shangaan-Tsonga the *shotso* or *rikhotso;* this is the heavy trunk of a tree, into which two holes have been carved, big enough to receive the two feet and legs of the patient. Two other small lateral holes are bored and a little, but solid, twig, introduced so that the person cannot withdraw his legs. I saw this with my own eyes in Gazaland, a very clever replica of the straight jacket. But again, this was applied only to the dangerous mentally disordered cases.[30]

When Africans did seek help for a mentally distressed relative, they rarely sought out Western psychiatric treatment as a first resort. The evidence overwhelmingly points to African antipathy toward mental institutions. Some of this distaste is powerfully conveyed in *Black Hamlet*. When Wulf Sachs first suggested hospitalization for the deranged Mawa, John Chawafambira and his wife, Maggie, both recoiled, accusing Sachs: "But you know that the white people don't understand the mad natives. They keep them there to die." Appalled by his encounter with the institutions of European psychiatry when he visited Weskoppies, "the terrible hospital" in Pretoria, John was convinced that it was the monstrous conditions in the hospital that caused the misery and anguish he witnessed there.[31] The authors of the Report of the Mental Hospital Departmental Committee, set up in 1936 to investigate conditions in the institutions, found a similar attitude among Africans, observing that "natives are reluctant to send relatives to mental institutions."[32]

This wariness, however, should not be equated with hostility toward Western medicine per se. On the contrary, by the 1930s, largely due to urbanization and high levels of morbidity, growing numbers of Africans came to accept Western biomedicine as part of their armory against ill health. They sought out its cures as part of a wider quest for therapy, most particularly for problems such as cataract removal and infant and maternal health care, where it had proved effective, thereby selectively incorporating certain biomedical concepts and practices within their healing strategies.[33]

Western psychiatric medicine, however, did not fall into this category, even if African healers certainly began to adopt psychiatric terminology such as *insanity* or *hysteria* in advertising their skills and treatments. One Charlie Fukela Nkele, a "medicine man" from Engcobo, claimed to be able to treat "insanity," "hysteria," and epileptic fits as well as fever, rheumatism, diarrhea, "kafir poison" [*sic*], and ailments of the womb.[34]

On the whole, there were strong disincentives to seeking psychiatric help from mental hospitals. They were viewed as impersonal and alien institutions, in comparison to treatment with traditional healers, whose task it was to get to know as much as possible about the patient's social situation, and thereby determine the illness of the individual, personally and socially.[35] In African societies, satisfactory healing was directed toward achieving social and psychological reintegration of patients and their community. By contrast, the barriers of language and culture in mental hospitals meant that only the most cursory of details were ever taken from African inmates. Stripped of their personal identities and social supports, they were reduced to a psychiatric classification and subjected to further depersonalization by the regime and rhythms of a "total institution." It is little wonder, then, that African men and women sought solace and support for their mentally ill outside the state psychiatric institutions. Even in Johannesburg in the 1950s, one anthropologist was struck by the "many psychological conditions caused by superstition, anxiety and fear among Africans, which are not understood by European doctors and which African doctors [healers] can, and do, cure."[36]

Much research on changing conceptions and healing of mental disorders in twentieth-century African societies is still needed. A vast literature exists about changing Western psychiatric practices, about the constant abandonment of old classifications and their replacement by "new" disorders. Similarly, it is clear from anthropological accounts that although Africans continuously sought out "traditional" cures for their mentally distressed, both the cultural expressions and treatments of behavioral and affective disorders changed markedly in the first three decades of this century under the impact of shattering social change associated with intensified migrancy and urbanization. The attendant upheaval, the rupturing of families and societies, the anomie, racial exclusion, and fierce competition for work, shelter, and security in the towns, the emergence of generation and gender tensions within households all threw up new challenges and traumas calling for novel existential answers.

The new forms of spirit possession, such as *indiki* and *ufufunyane*, that diffused through Natal, Zululand, and Mozambique in the first three decades of the twentieth century and the spread of faith-healing movements under the auspices of independent churches such as the Zionist Christian churches are among the better-known examples of these innovations. Both offered means of handling the psychic traumas of a rapidly changing way of life, and both displayed an eclecticism that reflected widened intellectual and experiential horizons of their participants. According to Harriet Ngubane, unlike the benign ukuthwasa, which befell those called on to become diviners, the emergence of the new "dangerous afflictions" of ufufunyane and indiki were linked to psychogenic disorders and were directly associated with the pressures of industrialism, migrancy, and urban immigration.[37] Possession cults concerned alien spirits who take over a host's body and whose general characteristics include those of "otherness" and individuality.[38] Among the Zulu, the *amandiki* were thought to be the restless spirits of those who had died away from home and were not accorded a proper burial, whereas for the Tsonga the spirits were believed to be the alien spirits of Zulu or Nguni warriors who had raided Mozambique under the reign of Gungunyana in the late nineteenth century. Indiki is described as derangement caused by the entry of a male spirit into a sufferer's chest, and only a diviner who has once been possessed by this spirit is deemed to be capable of exorcising and replacing it with an ancestral male spirit, who will protect the sufferer from future attacks. In some cases, indiki can engender healing and prophetic powers in the afflicted person, who might become a full-fledged diviner.

Patrick Harries has argued that the spread of indiki spirit possession, largely among women in Swaziland, Northern Zululand, and the eastern Transvaal from the late nineteenth century was akin to the waves of hysteria that swept through the industrialized world at the same time.[39] Its spread should likewise be understood as a consequence of tensions produced by rapid changes in the normal flow of life. The intensification of, and shift to, large-scale migrancy resulted in the increased domestic workload of women, their greater responsibility within the home, enforced sexual asceticism, and a state of insecurity engendered by anxiety about whether male homestead members would continue to send wages home or return on the completion of their contracts.

A whole range of tensions and unarticulated female aggressions triggered by the sharpening of patriarchal authority unleashed themselves through the medium of a possessing spirit. Spirit possession, for Harries, was both a protest made by women against their disadvantaged position and power-lessness, and a means of exerting emotional control within the family. The foreign spirit was a metaphor for the alien forces that had destabilized society, but, if correctly propiti-ated and controlled, could be of benefit to the society. The homestead head would have to demonstrate concern for the victim by procuring the services of an exorcist. In achieving a cure for the woman, the male had to accept her new status and power as an initiate of a spirit possession cult. Membership of this cult thereby provided women and disadvantaged males with an alternative political structure that was both a mutual aid group and an arena for individual advancement.

In the later waves of indiki, Ngubane likewise notes the underlying social tensions, arguing that indiki possession emerged among Zulu-speaking societies as a means of con-taining the threats posed by temporary relationships formed between alien migrants and Zulu women. Although the result-ing benefits to women are less clear cut, here the alien male is rejected and replaced by a male ancestor, which symbolizes what Ngubane describes as "the desired pattern of behavior."

Ufufunyane is also a condition known to cause deranged and frenzied behavior. As a consequence of sorcery, a sufferer is invaded by the spirits of different racial groups. The di-viner's task in such cases is to drive out the spirits, which then seek out other bodies insufficiently protected against them. As with indiki, Ngubane argues, this form of spirit possession is directly linked to the intense competition for work, shelter, and security that confronted Zulu migrants and urban immi-grants in the cities: "the thousands of spirits of various races that are believed to possess an ufufunyane sufferer and show their presence by violent aggression, hysteria or threat of sui-cide, indicate the social disorder which has led to many forms of social deprivation of the indigenous peoples in an unequal society."[40]

A significant characteristic of the new cults was that they were virtually restricted to women, who, once treated, would be inducted into a female cult group in which members would regularly undergo the possession experience. Like Harries, some writers see these cults as reactions of women to their subordinate position within society, as "thinly disguised protest movements against the dominant sex."[41]

As new afflictions emerged, so did healers who specialized in their treatment, giving rise to new guilds and cults in town and countryside. A range of other healers and herbalists also rose to these challenges. The reputation of Qobo Dhlamini, for example, who claimed an expertise in treating ufufunyane, spread far beyond the Natal town of Estcourt, where he practiced. As one of his supporters informed the Secretary for Public Health in June 1932, "many natives have been saved by him from entering the Mental Asylum and his powers in this direction are known throughout Natal." Moreover, Dhlamini was evidently particularly effective in ministering to people suffering from "native poisoning, treating others with dangerous instruments, screaming, swearing, doing many funny things not likely of being done by anyone except in cases of insanity." He regularly treated mentally suffering patients threatening to murder other Africans. If the authorities declined to renew Dhlamini's license to practice (as a licensed medicine man) as they threatened, "many Native patients shall enter the Mental Asylum," warned one A. F. Matibela.[42]

These examples point to the ways that mentally troubled individuals sought treatments and help outside the ambit of Western psychiatry and state mental hospitals. However, it is also the case that the numbers of African inmates in mental hospitals rose dramatically in the first four decades of the twentieth century. Although Africans rarely sent their "mildly disordered and harmless" relatives to mental hospitals, under the strain of urban existence particularly, the coping mechanisms of countless households had reached the breaking point by the early 1930s, with many despairing people bringing their seriously disturbed relatives or neighbors to the mental hospitals. Perhaps the last straw was uncontainable violence or a psychotic episode. Moreover, affected families in both town and country were often compelled by economic straits.[43] Together with the emotional and psychic stresses brought about by rapid social change, one of the factors likely to have lain behind the increased recourse to asylums is the rupturing of social and welfare networks, many of which underlay collective and social measures to combat illnesses.

The Path to Madness

When considering Nontetha's path to the asylum, it is clear that the stakes were heavily loaded against her. In the first place, the structure of law and authority in the Ciskei weighed in. According to the Native Administration Act of 1927, certain limited powers were extended to chiefs and headmen and certain customary law was binding on all Africans. Although they were expected to act as part of a colonial surveillance system, a chief's powers did not include civil or criminal jurisdiction. Criminal cases were referred to the nearest magistrates' court. In 1923 the Native Affairs Department appointed a Chief Native Commissioner for the Cape, based in King William's Town. The reserves of the Cape between the Fish and Kei Rivers were demarcated into magisterial districts, each under the jurisdiction of a Native Commissioner or magistrate presiding over a Native Commissioner's Court.[44]

It was this system of justice and power in which Nontetha found herself entangled by late 1922. Magistrates, the South African Police, officials in the Native Affairs Department, as well as headmen and location residents hostile to Nontetha's mission transmitted information about her actions among themselves in a series of telegrams, letters, eyewitness statements, and telephone calls. By themselves, they undoubtedly fanned official anxieties about her, culminating in her arrest in December 1922.

In cases such as Nontetha's, when a defendant was suspected by the court of being of unsound mind, a trial would be postponed in order to ascertain the state of the defendant's mind. The law made careful provision for doing so, as well as for sequestering the individual suspected of being "unsound of mind" in asylums. The Mental Disorders Act of 1918 empowered magistrates, courts, or judges, backed up by two medical certificates, to order the detention of a person suspected of being mentally disordered.[45]

From her first encounter with the legal system, followed by the medical examination ordered to ascertain her mental state, Nontetha's path to the mental hospital was set. Under other circumstances, the medical practitioners who interviewed her might have judged an illiterate African woman claiming to be an instrument of God as a harmless fanatic. Perhaps they would have regarded her behavior and declamations as evidence of the "normal" madness of credulous Africans. But because Nontetha's growing prominence as a prophet followed so closely on the heels of the Bulhoek massacre, she could not be thus disregarded. It can be imagined, too, that if the doctors observing Nontetha needed any reminder of the power of prophets in the eastern Cape, or the disruptive potential of an African "lunatic" at large, they needed only look at the chanting crowds of Nontetha's followers who had protectively encircled the King William's Town courthouse.

Fort Beaufort Mental Hospital

Fort Beaufort Mental Hospital, which Nontetha entered in December 1922, had changed little since 1894, when the empty military barracks at Fort Beaufort and the Lock Hospital were converted into the first exclusively black mental hospital in the Cape. Until then, the two Cape asylums on Robben Island and in Grahamstown had catered to black and white patients, albeit in segregated wards and with differential treatment and living conditions on the basis of race, class, gender, and mental disorder.[46] As pauper-patients, Africans invariably found themselves at the lowest rung in the hierarchy of treatments and conditions offered in these institutions. Preceded by the establishment by the exclusively white Valkenberg Mental Hospital in Cape Town, Fort Beaufort was established at a moment when comprehensive institutional and residential segregation was put in place in the Cape and when Africans in the eastern Cape were committed to asylums in unprecedented numbers. The opening of its doors to African patients was thus welcomed by the officials in other Cape asylums. As the superintendent of the Grahamstown asylum crowed, the establishment of the Fort Beaufort asylum "should enable us to get rid of all our Native patients."[47]

State psychiatry in South Africa, as elsewhere, was condemned to a lowly status within the medical system and mental hospitals were less than generously provisioned from state resources, resulting in chronic shortages and overcrowding of institutions up to and beyond the mid-twentieth century. And within the mental health system, facilities, services, and care for black—Asian, Coloured, and African—patients were inferior in all respects. Neither did the promulgation of the Mental Disorders Act of 1918 redress this racial imbalance. Although the act, like all the lunacy legislation that preceded it, did not specify the apportionment of resources or treatment along racial

lines, historical precedent and the orientation of the new state
Department of Mental Hygiene toward serving the needs of
the white population ensured that these differences deepened
further.

As a "native institution," from its earliest days, Fort Beaufort's management was governed by a policy of cost-cutting
with minimal regard to the health and well-being of the inmates. Moreover, the provision of inferior facilities for African
patients was justified by a psychiatric discourse that portrayed
the black mentally ill as more primitive, childish, and impervious to care than white patients. When additional accommodation was required for 100 male patients in 1907, a thatched
wattle-and-daub location annex was constructed for the purpose. The asylum authorities took pride in the savings of
£7,000 achieved, and in its "picturesque appearance," claiming
that traditional huts were preferred by African inmates.[48]

Even though they may well have been correct in this assertion, overcrowding, desperately inadequate food and sanita-
tion, and the absence of full-time medical supervision meant
that these new quarters rapidly became a squalid death trap.
The high incidence of scurvy, tuberculosis, and enteritis, which
characterized the asylum's early years, continued to scandal-
ize visitors and inspectors in the 1910s and 1920s. In just two
years, between 1916 and 1918, over half the patient deaths were
due to tuberculosis. So appalling were conditions in 1913 that
the parliamentary select committee on mental hospitals called
for the closure of this asylum, together with those at Robben
Island and Port Alfred. "These were not asylums at all," observed one psychiatrist, but "unsuitable places of detention . . .
dangerous to the mental and often to the physical welfare of
the patients."[49]

From its inception, Fort Beaufort always contained a large
number of chronic and incurable patients, who, complained the
Inspector of Asylums in 1907, "are long resident, occupy the

place of more urgent cases, and lead to overcrowding." Relatively few acute or recent cases were ever sent there, a factor which highlights the pre-eminently custodial function the hospital continued to serve in the twentieth century.[50] This tendency, and thus, image, of Fort Beaufort as a place of confinement for hopeless, incurable cases was reinforced with the establishment in 1922 of Komani Mental Hospital in Queenstown which received most of the new and acute African patients.

Although proposals had been made to convert Fort Beaufort into a hospital for chronic patients, these were scuppered during the First World War. The financial constraints of the war and postwar years, combined with the low priority given to the provision of adequate services for black patients, meant that little improvement was effected in the interwar years. In 1918, however, a tubercular shelter for female patients was built, and additional female wards were constructed in the late 1930s. Overall the dismal conditions in the hospital remained essentially unchanged for over a decade, leading the Orenstein Committee of 1936 to echo the concerns of the 1913 select committee about the institution's insalubrious and overcrowded state. Overcrowding, the committee noted, was the major obstacle that stood in the way of patients' recovery.

Evidence abounds about the parsimony that shaped the administrative and medical regimes at Fort Beaufort. The daily cost of maintaining a patient at Fort Beaufort in 1923, for example, stood at 1s 11d, the lowest cost per patient amongst the Union's eight mental hospitals. By contrast, the daily cost per patient stood 3s 8d at Grahamstown, at 2s 10d at Valkenberg, and 2s 7d at the Pretoria Mental Hospital.[51] The financial strains were particularly acute, given the fact that virtually all patients came from poor families who could not contribute to their maintainence. In 1920, the hospital succeeded in recovering a derisory £96 from patients' relatives. Medication appears not to have been widely available in the institution, as this would have substantially increased running costs. Difficult or psychotic patients were more likely to have been placed into "seclusion." Savings were also made in the appointment of staff. In keeping with South Africa's racial hierarchy, the senior staff such as matrons, sisters, and staff nurses were all white and were required to pass examinations administered by the Medical Psychological Association. They were thus relatively expensive. But there was no full-time psychiatrist employed at Fort Beaufort in this period and anecdotal evidence suggests that little care was given in the appointment of other hospital employees. According to one account, other white staff members had no prior training in the treatment and handling of the mentally ill, and were often former soldiers or farmers.[52] The black nurses (eleven out of twenty-four nurses in 1923) employed by the institution are more properly described as untrained assistants who were consigned to the most menial labor in the institution and to the trying tasks of ensuring the patients remained clean and dry. The nature of their work, their pitiful remuneration, and the fact that they were temporary appointments can hardly have made their jobs anything but demoralizing; compassion and patience for their wards would have been difficult to maintain under such conditions.

Diagnosis and Control

For some glimpse of Nontetha's experiences in Fort Beaufort Mental Hospital over a two-year period, we are compelled to rely on a retrospective psychiatric report and on some oral testimony. From these sources, we know that Nontetha remained adamant that she had been divinely inspired. She told her psychiatric interlocutors that "God had picked her to preach to the natives because all their sins would rest on her if she did not." He had entered her blood and placed writing in her head that she could read and understand. One account describes Nontetha preaching, looking into her hands, reading messages from them in much the way we know she did when conducting her outdoor services in her home area. According to the hospital staff, she would stand and preach over a fence "to nobody in particular" or pray over patients. Her preaching on many occasions is described as vehement, passionate, militant, noisy, and hostile, which the psychiatrists interpreted as signs of "religious exaltation" accompanied by "acute and constant hallucinosis." They concluded that Nontetha was delusional (see appendix, document 2).[53]

The same document reports that Nontetha was convinced that the doctors were withholding a letter addressed to her from "the father of Queen Victoria" and that she had vowed to continue preaching and singing until it was returned to her. On one occasion in December 1924, she evidently claimed that Queen Victoria herself had communicated with her and had told her that "everything she, Nontete, says is true." She also became convinced that the Fort Beaufort staff was trying to poison her.

When first examined in 1922, Nontetha was diagnosed with dementia praecox, of the hebephrenic type,[54] a now obsolete term for schizophrenia. Whereas mania in the late nineteenth century was the most frequently used classification for African asylum inmates in South Africa, in the early twentieth century, this designation was replaced by dementia. According to an influential British textbook of the day, hebephrenia was distinguished by great incoherence of thought, was marked by emotional disturbances, periods of wild excitement, tearful periods, and depression, and was often accompanied by illusions and particularly vivid hallucinations of sight and hearing that would come and go in the course of the illness. The most pronounced symptoms were identified as incoherent thinking; strange, impulsive, senseless conduct; and vivid hallucinations.[55]

It can readily be seen how it was possible for Nontetha's otherwise incomprehensible actions to be matched by psychiatrists with the symptoms of dementia praecox. In their report, the psychiatrists do not make any specific reference to Nontetha's "race" or culture, and the relationship of these factors to her conditions, as might be expected from members of a profession which largely agreed on the essential differences between black and white psychopathology. Without further information at our disposal, we may infer that however "other" Nontetha appeared to them, these doctors accepted a rough equivalence between African and white presentations of symptoms.[56]

At the time, the prognosis for schizophrenic disorders was not a hopeful one; the majority of patients were expected to steadily deteriorate and thus were considered to be best cared for in a mental hospital. This pessimistic view about the likelihood of Nontetha's recovery was doubtless strengthened when her conditional release in 1923 ended in her rearrest and recommittal to Fort Beaufort. While prospects for recovery were remote, it was believed that readjustment could be assisted through a combination of bed rest, occupational therapy, and outdoor work under hospital conditions. The soothing environment of the quiet, orderly mental hospital, with its reassuring discipline, tolerant and understanding staff, and its simplified life, could produce some change. Good bodily health, nourishing food, and sufficient sleep were essential to creating a state of betterment. However, while it is to be doubted that such an ideal was ever realized in British hospitals, it was certainly at odds with the squalor and cacophony of the African wards of South African mental hospitals. Moreover, by the second decade of the twentieth century, with the problems caused by overcrowding, the mental hospitals preferred to discharge African patients who were not dangerous, rather than keep them confined indefinitely.

In the absence of complete case records for Nontetha—or, indeed, for other patients—it is not possible to reconstruct her routine and treatment during her two-year stint in Fort Beaufort. One of the reasons for the difficulty in providing a picture of Nontetha's immediate environment is that the Fort Beaufort female asylum where she was confined was a completely separate institution located a quarter of a mile away from the male asylum, which served as the administrative center of the institution as a whole. The official records focus mainly on the larger male asylum, reflecting a general lack of interest in providing care for mentally ill black women. Annual reports from the period and accounts from the 1940s, however, offer some glimpses of hospital life and into the ways in which conformity to institutional codes and rhythms were inculcated through dress and routine. Most powerfully, they shed light on the sheer poverty and neglect in that institution.

Contemporary accounts point to the wretchedness of conditions of the female asylum. Although it was considerably smaller and less crowded than the male asylum (152 female as opposed to 425 male patients in 1923), it shared the latter's high rates of infectious diseases such as typhoid, and the incidence of tuberculosis was reported to be considerably higher in the female asylum. Nontetha would have shared a spartan dormitory with mainly chronic, long-term patients, the majority of whom were elderly and in poor health. Also, given the nature and seriousness of their disorders, there would have been frequent scuffles, conflicts, and explosions of tension among the women.

Nontetha's daily routine was likely to have been an extremely monotonous one. Well before breakfast at 7 A.M., patients were dressed (in standard khaki dresses, but not shoes or underwear) and shepherded into the courtyards outdoors where they spent their days, watched over by the nursing staff. Inmates spent long hours outside in the heat or cold, remaining indoors in dormitories only in the event of rain. Meals were served outside on the veranda at wooden benches and tables, and patients were bathed once a week. Despite repeated requests, there was neither a day room nor dining room in the female asylum during Nontetha's time, and unlike the male asylum, no sporting or other leisure activities were provided. Other than daily walks and light gardening, Nontetha might have been assigned the work of chopping stones to make gravel paths for the institution's grounds. It is to be wondered whether she was dosed with a preparation of paraldehyde, chloral hydrate, and bromide, the medication administered to restless and "noisy" patients.[57] We do know that she was isolated at least on one occasion in the airing garden when she had become "noisy and hostile." The general practice of seclusion at Fort Beaufort involved locking up psychotic patients in a room with a coir mattress on the floor, where they were left until they became calmer. Although there were clear procedures for this practice and for monitoring patients, it was one which was open to abuse by overworked and demoralized staff.

In Fort Beaufort, as in other "total institutions" in South Africa, control and order were ensured through a range of strategies, and not by repression alone.[58] It is clear, for example, that a complex hierarchy of privileges and special rights for certain patients, particularly in relation to food, were negotiated with the asylum authorities and staff and that this was as essential in maintaining order and discipline in the institution as were more overt forms of punishment, isolation, and restraint. Thus, when new staff members intervened in the "old rights" of Fort Beaufort patients in January 1943, aggrieved patients armed themselves with tools and broken furniture, rioted, burned blankets, and attacked the staff and other patients.[59] Such glimpses reveal that even if reciprocal obligations and duties were negotiated between some patients and some staff, and even if spaces for conviviality between some patients were carved out, violence and the threat of violence were a constant feature of institutional life at Fort Beaufort.

Despite being deprived of her liberty at Fort Beaufort, Nontetha was never entirely cut off from the world she had known outside the asylum. Her followers remained intensely devoted to her, visiting her repeatedly during 1923 and 1924 and deferring to her authority and leadership. The hospital authorities, however, took a dim view of their constant presence. On the pretext that the visits were too disruptive to the hospital regime, Nontetha was sent to Pretoria (Weskoppies) Mental Hospital on 4 December 1924.[60] Transferring African patients from one mental hospital to another was an unusual step, particularly at a time when institutions objected to shouldering the costs of such transfers. A strong case would have to have been made to secure Nontetha's removal, for which there were no medical grounds, to Weskoppies in Pretoria, where she had no kin. The decision was taken without consulting her family, and her followers were told by the Fort Beaufort officials only that she had left and that her whereabouts were unknown. These facts suggest that Nontetha was removed to Weskoppies because the authorities were determined to bring an end to the movement by totally severing her from her followers. When Nontetha's family and followers finally traced her to Weskoppies, officials there forbade them from visiting her. They told them that their presence would exacerbate her condition.[61]

Weskoppies

Conditions in the *Krankzinnigengesticht* (lunatic asylum) in Pretoria, founded in 1892 by the Transvaal administration, were the subject of a minor scandal during the South African War (1899–1902) when the occupying British power removed the incumbent staff and took over the running of the institution. Maladministration, corruption, inadequate methods of care, and abominable living conditions were the main charges laid against the former Dutch superintendent physician of the asylum. In a report on the institution in 1901, the new British superintendent, Dr. Todd, found it "difficult to find the words to express the state of the Institution and its inmates or where to commence." In the main building of the hospital, which accommodated white patients—"a warren of dark passages, cells and small damp yards"—all patients, curable and incurable, were herded together. Beyond the main building, in the outbuildings and yards for African patients, Todd found: "their airing court was a sort of farm yard in which were found 11 pigs, 4 goats, fowls and several dogs. The lower part of the yard was a network of wire used for drying the Asylum washing. The upper part [was] overgrown with grass in which I found heaps of faeces and filth of every description."[62]

On taking over the running of the asylum, Dr. Todd was determined to overhaul it in accordance with "modern" asylum management conventions in England. Like the asylums of the British Raj of an earlier age, and prestige institutions such as the Grahamstown or Valkenberg asylums, it was to display the humanitarian ethos and scientific progress that proponents claimed to lie at the heart of British imperialism, ideological values consistent with the political and economic reconstruction of the war-ravaged Transvaal under Lord Milner.[63] In 1906 two British-trained physicians, Drs. J. T. Dunston and

Egerton Brown, were appointed to the hospital. By 1907 most of the old and dilapidated buildings were demolished and replaced by the bow-windowed, red-brick Edwardian buildings that continue to serve as wards and administrative offices of Weskoppies in the 1990s. Based on the architectural principles of Menston Hospital in Yorkshire (and making no concessions to local climatic conditions, such as providing verandas or shelter from the fierce highveld sun), it was planned to accommodate 430 patients.[64] In the following two years, the original wood-and-iron outhouses that had continued to house African patients were demolished and replaced with solid-stone buildings, but once again, resolutely apart from white wards and facilities. In accordance, too, with the ideal of an asylum as a pastoral refuge, over the next decade some two thousand trees and a luxuriant garden were planted, transforming the stark buildings and the bare koppie into what was, in some respects, a lush retreat.

By 1924, when Nontetha was transferred to Pretoria, Weskoppies was a changed institution, and vastly different from the impoverished Fort Beaufort asylum. The transformation, moreover, went beyond the physical improvement of the buildings and estate. Serving the population of the most industrialized and populous region of the country, and situated in its economic hub and political center, by the 1920s the hospital had gained a reputation as a center of innovation and research. Its medical practitioners took pride in keeping pace with the advances in international psychiatric medicine. In 1923 the hospital pioneered malarial treatment of general paralysis of the insane (GPI, the terminal phase in syphilis) in South Africa; and, in 1937, it introduced insulin shock therapy for the treatment of dementia praecox. It had also become the training hospital for the University of the Witwatersrand medical students, as well as a school for mental health nurses.[65] By this time, the physician superintendent of Weskoppies, Dr. J. T.

Dunston, had become a nationally respected figure in eugenist and psychiatric circles, as well as the government's Commissioner for Mental Hygiene.[66] If Fort Beaufort was an obscure, backwater institution, Weskoppies was, at least on paper, the epitome of scientific modernity. Needless to say, the benefits of its much-vaunted "advances" bypassed the African wards.

Originally, only limited provision had been made for African patients, but in the early decades of the twentieth century, higher numbers of black patients than expected were institutionalized. In 1901 there were 85 male and 18 female African patients. By 1916 the 289 black patients constituted 57 percent of the total inmate population. Twenty years later, of a total of 1,663 patients, 761 were black—537 men and 224 women.[67]

In many respects, Weskoppies had become a transit station for mentally ill African migrants and immigrants who had made their way from all corners of southern Africa to the gold mines and towns of the Witwatersrand in search of better opportunities, higher wages, and the imagined freedoms of urban existence. African patients brought with them a multitude of regional cultures, practices, and languages, and thus must have presented Nontetha with a dazzling contrast to the relative linguistic and cultural homogeneity of the small Fort Beaufort hospital. Migrant miners who went insane in the compounds or in the mining stopes were dispatched at the mines' expense to Pretoria Mental Hospital for observation and thereafter discharged to the care of their rural kin if they were considered to be sufficiently recovered.[68] A fairly typical story is that of "Native Sixpence" Malele who was arrested and sent to Weskoppies for observation after suddenly becoming violent in Witbank in June 1927. He was soon discharged, the doctors at Weskoppies having decided that his "weakness" was of "a temporary and intermittent nature."[69] Africans from the jails and Native Commissioners' courts of the Transvaal reserves, from Swaziland, Namibia, and elsewhere were sent to Weskoppies, as were the criminally insane and Governor-General's patients. The latter were those convicted of crimes of violence, such as rape, assault, murder, and arson.[70]

Increasingly, as one staff member observed in the 1930s, the inmate population were residents from the locations, slum yards, and shantytowns of the Witwatersrand and Pretoria rather than from the "rural kraals," a factor that fueled the idea that African insanity was a consequence of "town evils"— dagga smoking, liquor, women, and venereal diseases.[71] Undoubtedly, the strains of urban life did contribute to the rising numbers of Africans entering the mental health system.

In straitened economic circumstances, in intensely overcrowded rooms, shanties, and houses in the segregated locations or city slums in a situation where only minimal social welfare was provided, African families and households were likely to have struggled to care for their insane relatives. Some charitable and mission institutions attempted to intervene and offer assistance. Miss Dorothy Maud and the missionaries of the Anglican Church Mission at Ekutuleni in the Sophiatown township were one such group commended for their "great work with the native people" and to whom Native Affairs officials turned with problematic cases of African mental patients.[72] But, as noted earlier, insane Africans who could be cared for by neither their families nor charitable organizations, and whose own social networks and safety networks failed them, found themselves incarcerated in the Pretoria Hospital in growing numbers by the second and third decades of the twentieth century.

After her transfer to Weskoppies, Nontetha continued to preach to those around her and to insist that she was a prophet, directly inspired by God. She was observed by the staff of this institution to enter states of "religious exaltation" and excitement and to have "delusions" of a "grandiose" and "persecutory" nature. At Weskoppies, as at Fort Beaufort, she was also described as having violent episodes, as being aggressive and attacking patients for no reason "apart from her disordered promptings."[73]

From the perspective of the hospital staff, Nontetha, with her visions and zealous commitment to her prophesying mission, was no different, in her detachment from reality, from the many King Georges, Gods, Satans, chiefs, and chief magistrates who peopled the hospital wards. Many other patients claimed divine inspiration, too: "Christ came to me last night," one inmate told John Chawafambira. "He told me that I was chosen to punish all the white people." Although such claims could be dismissed as harmless delusions, they were probably extremely unsettling for hospital staff. For with their visions and posturings, and their taking on the persona of powerful or biblical figures, mad African patients focused uncomfortable attention on existing relations of power.[74]

Nontetha's fervent desire to be allowed to communicate with Queen Victoria, her sense of persecution, and her commitment to her prophetic mission may be a case in point. The image and idea of Queen Victoria was a resonant and powerful one in African thought. Liberator of the slaves, embodiment of British justice, and guardian of equality before the law of all subjects of the empire, Queen Victoria was a potent symbol for Africans who sought greater political freedoms in late-nineteenth- and early-twentieth-century South Africa. She was the standard against which subsequent administrations that turned their backs on this vision were held. Richard Selope Thema, for example, recalled in 1925 that he had come to "admire British institutions of justice." Childhood stories told to him by his father about "a Great White Queen across the seas who made no distinction between white and black in the administration of her laws" made a powerful impression on him.[75] The symbol of Queen Victoria could also be given a specifically feminist slant. As late as 1937, during Margaret Ballinger's campaign for election as a parliamentary Native Representative in the eastern Cape, her supporters argued in support of her candidature that it had been a woman, Queen Victoria, who gave Africans political rights, and the men who had taken them away.[76]

A symbolic reading of Nontetha's invocation of Queen Victoria, and her complaint against the authorities for withholding her letter, renders Victoria an icon of liberty, justice, and support for suppressed colonial peoples, and therefore serves as a comment on the injustice of her own confinement. It is also possible to read Nontetha's insistence on preaching "to no-one in particular" as an act of defiance against the authorities that sought to thwart her religious calling. In the light of what we know about the living conditions and disciplinary regimes in mental hospitals, we might also consider that there was some substance to her "paranoid" representations and feelings of persecution. Consider, for example, her claim to being poisoned and burned by the doctors. An alternative reading might suggest her revulsion at unfamiliar and unpalatable institutional food, or her experience of her incarceration at the hands of the doctors as their willful and malicious attempt to foil her mission to Christianize and thereby redeem her society.

There simply is not the evidence available to offer anything more than this tentative interpretation. Whether or not Nontetha was mad is a question that cannot be answered, and in any event, it is less significant to this study than are the perceptions and decisions of the psychiatrists. Whereas Nontetha's behavior and actions had not been deemed aberrant, even by her opponents within the world of Ciskeian locations, within the mental hospital (where only the mentally disordered spoke to themselves, or opened their hands as if reading from a book) Nontetha's actions and demeanor continuously confirmed the psychiatrists' diagnosis of her as psychotic. Considering her accusations of the hospital staff burning her or withholding her letters from (long deceased) members of the British royal family, the psychiatrists would undoubtedly have classed Nontetha as "a certain type of patient" who routinely made "the wildest and most preposterous and unfounded accusations against the medical officers, the nursing staff, and the [Hospital] Board collectively and individually." This attitude, combined with the psychiatrists' utter unfamiliarity with Xhosa culture, language, symbol, and metaphor, as well as the problems inherent in the process of translation, meant that they could only take on face value the literal meanings of her utterances as translated to them by interpreters.

Despite labeling Nontetha as a victim of persecutory and delusional fantasies, the hospital authorities were well aware of her capacity for charismatic leadership in the outside world. And it was that preoccupation, rather than concern for her well-being, that lay behind the decision to keep Nontetha confined. When Dunston was forced by public pressure to reassess Nontetha's case in 1928, he conceded that she did not represent a danger or threat to anyone. But, "wherever she goes," he pronounced, "she will create a disturbance and cause trouble." For those reasons, he could not consent to her release. He also claimed that the visits of her relatives and disciples exacerbated her condition, and he forbade them from visiting her (see appendix, document 1).[77]

Between 1929 and 1930 the hospital report suggests that Nontetha was calmer. For long periods, she showed no "aggressive violence." Her demeanor was subdued, and she was in reasonable physical health. Nevertheless, the same report indicates that she had begun to show signs of distress and agitation. Early in 1930 she was noted to have been restless, to be sleeping badly, and to have lost her appetite. She nevertheless remained "deluded," clinging to her belief that she was being burned on the right side of her body. This last assessment of Nontetha was made in May 1930. It was prompted by officials from the Native Affairs Department, who were responding to mounting publicity over Nontetha's continued incarceration.

540	87	650	Conrad Edward Appel	120 Van Buchholz Ave. Pta	20.5.35
541	88	341	Martha Mahane	129 Koper Loc... Pta	20.5.35
542	89	653	Polly Jonas	Jootfolii...	21.5.35
543	90	656	Baaap Malambo	Jaat Pta	21.5.35
544	91	651	Beatrie Elizabeth Zwarman	Mental Hospital Pta	20.5.35
545	92	655	Daniel Hendrick Kleyn	Klerksdorp	21.5.35
546	93	654	Margaret Polley	230 Scheemanok. Pta	21.5.35
547	94		A.E. Polley	Polleys Hotel Pta	
548	95		Mrs Hutchison	91 P.Ly 360 Pta	
			A. Ham	90 P.Ly 360 Pta	
		8	Thomas Joseph Nelson	Jacula Pta	20.6.35
		657	Francis Adita Antoinetta Bonné	3rd Rebecca St Pta	21.5.35 Dist of Death
			Mrs J. Bapolik	90 P Ly 360 Ltd	
549	96	642	Nontetha	Mental Hospital Pta	20.5.35
			Mrs A. Mill	62 Nobi Rd ... Elizabeth	
			Mrs T.N. Fish	209 Katzen St. Pta	
550	97	659	Edwin Guillaume Atkins	258 Brook St. Brooklyn Pta	22.5.35
551	98	86	Charles Landos A. Rose	269 Rees St. Rees Street	23.5.35

Burial Register page for Nontetha, Newclare Cemetery, Pretoria

Elders of the Church of the Prophetess Nontetha in prayer before the commencement of the exhumation of Nontetha's grave. Bishop Mzwandile Mabhelu is on the right. *(Anton Hammerl)*

Tobi Nokrawuzana at exhumation of Nontetha's grave, Pretoria, July 1998 *(Anton Hammerl)*

Group at exhumation. Coen Nienaber digs in the background. Standing are Johan Green, Superintendent of Rebecca Street Cemetery, Nosabata Morley, eastern Cape provincial government official, Lulamile Leve, Tobi Nokrawuzana, Sitati Gitywa, government official, and Nontzapho Deleki, a granddaughter of Nontetha. *(Anton Hammerl)*

Tobi Nokrawuzana and another woman of Church of Prophetess
Nontetha at all-night vigil at Nontetha's casket, 25 October 1998
(Sally Gaulle)

Women at vigil at Nontetha's casket, 25 October 1998
(Sally Gaulle)

Mzwandile Mabhelu, Bishop of Church of Prophetess Nontetha, holding program for reburial service *(Lori Waselchuk)*

Members of church surround her casket at reburial service
(Lori Waselchuk)

Praise singer orates at funeral service *(Sally Gaulle)*

Procession from church to grave site *(Lori Waselchuk)*

Mourners at graveside ceremony at Nontetha's funeral
(Lori Waselchuk)

4

Pilgrimages of Grace

Through the night of doubt and sorrow
Onward goes the pilgrim band,
Singing songs of expectation,
Marching to the Promised Land
　　　—From a hymn by Sabine Baring-Gould

Nontetha's plight might have gone largely unnoticed had it not been for the actions of her loyal supporters and the publicity they generated. They tried to visit her but repeatedly were denied permission, so they took the initiative and organized several "pilgrimages of grace" to Pretoria, some six hundred miles away.[1] Although the journeys were intended to convince the government to release her, they also testify eloquently to the faith, dedication, and devotion of her followers.

Before they set out on foot on their first journey, on 23 November 1926, Nontetha instructed her followers not to bring along any provisions or to carry passes, "so that people could understand the power of God."[2] Nevertheless they provided themselves with a measure of security by taking along a total of £10. As the band of pilgrims trekked northward through the eastern Cape, they discovered the meaning of their prophet's words. They did not have to use their money; they subsisted on *utshongo* (roasted mealies), mealie meal and tea, and donations from sympathetic Africans and whites.

One of the pilgrims, Tobi Nokrawuzana, recollected a white

farmer in the Cape by the name of Charlie, who warned them not to cross a nearby mountain because snow was likely. If they pressed on anyway, he assured them he would have a place for them to sleep should they have to turn back (and even instructed them how to avoid dogs near his home). The group doubted his word because he was white; but when he turned out to be correct about the snow, they returned to his home. He had them chop firewood so they could make tea. After watching them praying for a whole day, Charlie asked them to pray for a servant of his who was critically ill. They sang and prayed over him and he recovered.[3]

When the pilgrims reached the Orange Free State, the men ran into problems with the police. African women were not required to carry passes in the Orange Free State, but African men were—and only seven of the male followers had them. The men were arrested in Rouxville and were jailed for two weeks. While they served their sentences, the rest of the group proceeded on. After they served their time, they were freed and issued passes; eventually they caught up with the main party near Vereeniging, in the Transvaal.

On their journey the pilgrims usually slept in bushes by the side of the road, but as they moved into the urbanized areas of the Witwatersrand, they slept on the outskirts of cities so that they would not be harassed for pass law violations. Indeed they calculated their arrival in Pretoria on a weekday, when they could go directly to government offices.

They finally arrived in Pretoria on the fifty-fifth day of their pilgrimage, in mid-January 1927. The day was memorable because as they marched through the streets singing, they attracted the attention of many black domestic servants, who left their kitchens unattended and burnt the meals of their European employers.

Weskoppies hospital officials decided to allow Nontetha's disciples to meet with her on 18 January at a reception depot near a black township administered by the Native Commissioner's Office. Nontetha was gratified that they had come because their act of sacrifice was proof that she could not be crazy. She prayed for them and preached about love and mercy; and she directed them to return to their homes to keep the movement alive. "They had to ask God to liberate them and allow them to rule their country according to their own nationhood." If her followers disagreed on issues, "they were to go to a grove near Gola's place; it was where she [Nontetha] had met God and where the final catastrophe would occur."[4]

At the Fort Beaufort hospital, Nontetha had accused officials of poisoning her food. Although she regained her health after being transferred to Weskoppies, she now claimed that Weskoppies officials were also poisoning her food because she refused to go along with a government ploy to keep her quiet by offering her a farm. She also said that hospital officials had tried to arrange a marriage with a Pretoria man in return for her silence.[5]

Her followers approached municipal officials in Pretoria to press for her release, but were informed that the British governor general had arrested her. When they asked where he was, they were told he was in England. While willing to march all the way to England for their cause, they settled for petitioning the king of England to release her.

Once it became apparent that Nontetha's supporters intended to stay in Pretoria indefinitely, government officials ordered them to leave. However, they had taken so much effort to travel to Pretoria that they were not prepared to leave unless Nontetha was released.[6] All were charged and convicted of violating a provision of the Urban Areas Act—entering the Transvaal without a pass. They were sentenced to fines of £2 or one month of jail with hard labor, but the state was prepared to suspend their sentences if they would leave. When they refused to comply, they had to serve their sentences and then were put on a train and shipped back under guard to King William's Town.[7] In April another group of seven followers arrived in Pretoria by train, and they were similarly charged with violating pass laws. When they agreed to return home, they were given suspended sentences.

Members of Nontetha's family were allowed to visit her in April 1928. They, too, lobbied for her release, but were rebuffed by Dr. Dunston, the Commissioner for Mental Hygiene, who ruled Nontetha was "not fit for discharge." Several delegations of Nontetha's supporters also approached the Chief Native Commissioner in King William's Town to ask for her release. He was sympathetic to their request and asked the superintendent of Weskoppies to review her case and look into the possibility of releasing her, providing no trouble should ensue. He concluded, "it will remove a sense of grievance which is felt by persons following a form of religion having much to commend it but which brought them into conflict with the law."[8]

In early 1930 Nontetha's disciples renewed their efforts to secure her release by launching a second "pilgrimage of grace" with about fifty Mtetes (as her disciples were known on this journey), including two of Nontetha's daughters, participating. Government officials tracked their progress northward and, in Jamestown, the group was warned that the Mtete men would not be issued passes to enter the Orange Free State. On 27 February on the outskirts of Aliwal North, an entry point for the Orange Free State, the Mtetes encountered police blocking the main road and railway bridge across the Orange River.

The Mtetes responded by camping out on the Aliwal North commonage, singing, and holding religious services. They received some material support and considerate treatment from several African and white organizations. Africans sympathetic to their plight wired the prime minister and the Minister of Native Affairs, requesting that Nontetha be released and reunited with her followers.[9]

After several weeks the patience of Aliwal North officials wore thin. On 10 February they warned the Mtetes to pack their belongings and leave by 5 P.M. the next day. The following morning, a procession of hymn-singing Mtetes, accompanied by a crowd of Aliwal North Africans, marched across the Orange River bridge, where a dozen police arrested the men for not having passes. The Mtetes offered no resistance. Nineteen men were sentenced to a fine or thirty days in jail. When no one paid, they were sent to the King William's Town jail to serve time.[10]

Since African women were not obligated to carry passes in the Orange Free State, thirty women disciples were allowed to proceed. However, they chose to remain near their men folk and congregated at the police camp and outside the magistrate's court at Aliwal North. When they ignored an order to leave, they were charged with trespassing and sentenced to thirty days in jail. Because there was not enough space in the King William's Town jail to accommodate them, they served their sentences in Middelburg.[11] Both the men and women were released in April and put on a train to Middledrift.[12]

The pilgrimages were widely covered in the African and white press. The Pretoria-based correspondent of the East London *Daily Dispatch* reported regularly on the progress of the pilgrimages and investigated Nontetha's situation in the mental hospital. Surprisingly the reports in the white press were sympathetic, if patronizing in tone. If anything, white journalists were intrigued and amused by "the crazy prophetess" and her adherents; if implicitly they accepted that Nontetha really was mad, they certainly did not portray her as a threat to state or national security. Commenting on reports that Nontetha continued to call herself a prophetess who had been inspired by God to deliver a message to her people, one such journalist wrote:

She says she is the earthly confidante of Queen Victoria, with whom, she says, she frequently converses. At first Nonteta's discontent at her separation from her people were [*sic*] intense, and she gave a certain amount of trouble to the authorities, but lately she has calmed down somewhat, and she is rather popular with the staff of the medical hospital. Now and again, she is once more inspired with her former fanatical self; sings, prays and preaches sermons, to which the native patients listen intently. Though these manifestations of her beliefs are not necessarily in accord with the religious feelings of their hearers, who welcome her outbursts as an entertainment rather than as a religious exercise.[13]

By this time, too, a few Africans began to challenge the government's rationale for confining Nontetha in a mental hospital. Calling on the government to release her, they questioned whether she actually posed a threat and proclaimed her right to express her own religious beliefs. For instance, D. W. Ntsikana, a grandson of the prophet Ntsikana and an independent church leader in his own right, penned a letter to Prime Minister Hertzog in which he asked: "Why should Nonteta be incarcerated in the asylum?" Ntsikana initially believed she had been arrested for disturbing the peace, but when he investigated her case, he learned that no chief had turned her over to the authorities for insanity or disloyalty. Why should she be arrested, he asked, if she were really a positive moral force in her community? "On studying her life closer I find that she had marvellous and remarkable powers of converting natives, the people lisped her name with gratitude, and her congregation grew by leaps and bounds, much to the exasperation, disgust and annoyance of other religious missionary bodies whose success is very slow. During her short working period she made many converts. Natives ceased their Kaffir beer traffic, stealing and robbing were put by, all this to the advantage of ourselves and the Government."

Ntsikana attributed her arrest to "wrong information" spread by white missionaries who were jealous of her success and the loss of their followings. He also criticized the government for violating her freedom to hold religious views, even if they ran counter to orthodox beliefs. "As a person who enjoys the freedom of the Union Jack I see no reason why I should be scorned at for my opinion, and likewise I see no reason why these people should not be allowed to enjoy freedom of worship." Ntsikana referred to religious groups in Europe that enjoyed religious freedom even though they were out of the mainstream.[14]

A follower of Nontetha, Delanto Qoshe, seconded this view when he questioned why the government could arrest her for her religious beliefs: "if you don't please point out the reason why you should not let her out because first Government sent out ministers of the Gospel to preach it among the people now when the prophetess also came by the same way you imprisoned her and said she's mad. Now I ask from our authorities to point us out what is truth and what is error because I think if what she preaches is an error the whole world must also be the same."[15]

The publicity generated sympathy across a range of African and white groups. Charles Crabtree, for example, the secretary of the Aliwal North Welfare Society and member of the Primitive Methodist Church, urged the Native Affairs Department to seek medical opinion to determine whether Nontetha should be released.[16] Crabtree hoped thereby that the impasse that had developed between Nontetha's supporters and the authorities could be broken. In turn, Native Affairs Department officials and the Aliwal North member for Parliament, Sephton, pressed the hospital to reassess Nontetha's mental condition.[17]

A Second Opinion

The hospital's superintendent, Dr. F. D. Crosthwaite, accordingly called a full conference in June 1930 to discuss Nontetha's history and prognosis. In her interviews with individual doctors, she was evidently unhappy, complaining that the doctors were causing her to be burned "day and night." The conference concluded that Nontetha was indeed mentally disordered and not merely a "religious fanatic." She was "undoubtedly the subject of aural, visual and sensory hallucinosis." Her general quiescence during the period of the interviews was believed to be due to the gradual onset of senility. The doctors thought it highly unlikely that Nontetha was capable of insight into her condition and that she would thus relinquish her "delusion" that she was a "directly inspired prophetess of God with a message for her own people, which none but she can deliver." Only such "insight" would have constituted a sign of recovery.

Although Nontetha's symptoms and behavior were described in essentially the same terms as they had been in earlier accounts, after this conference, Crosthwaite revised the Fort Beaufort diagnosis of "praecox sub-group Hebephrenia."[18] He argued that her symptoms did not conform to those normally associated with hebephrenia: "Mannerisms, Psychic Ataxia with senseless incomprehensible conduct," he suggested, and the sharp mood shifts characteristic of this disorder were notably absent in Nontetha. Her emotions seemed to him to correspond to the ideas she expressed. In his view, the states of mild depression that had been occasionally viewed were due to her thwarted desire for release. Alternatively, the depression was only apparent as the result of "temporary defervescence" (quieting down) of the religious exaltation. Crosthwaite concluded his diagnosis by classifying her "amongst the Paranoiacs, sub-group 'Prophets, Saints and Mystics' amongst whom visionary experiences are common."[19]

This classificatory fine-tuning, however, would make little difference to the psychiatric assessment of the likelihood of "recovery" in Nontetha's case. The prognosis of the day for paranoiacs differed little from that of patients with dementia praecox (hebephrenia). According to the authors of a standard textbook on psychiatry in this period, D. K. Henderson and R. D. Gillespie, paranoiacs usually declined into a state of dementia.[20] In their experience, only a small number who entered mental hospitals were ever capable of making sufficient readjustment to enable them to live outside again, let alone lead useful lives.

If her reclassification and its associated "therapeutic pessimism" did not enhance Nontetha's chances of release, neither did it make any difference to her "treatment." Indeed, as we will argue, it was not the purpose of the diagnostic procedure to proffer meaningful explanations to Nontetha of her plight or to offer therapeutic benefits, but rather to authorize her continued confinement. Moreover, the very acts of "labeling" Nontetha made it highly unlikely that the psychiatrists could view her through any other prism that would allow for a different perspective on either her mental state or her broader social role. Every action of Nontetha's merely served to prove the veracity of their diagnosis and classification.[21]

Although Crosthwaite considered it unlikely that Nontetha would be "any less tenacious" in clinging to her beliefs if released, he did not believe that she constituted a danger to herself.[22] In response to the question whether she should be allowed conditional discharge to specified relatives, he responded: "There is no reason why she should not be so discharged having regard only to her mental condition."[23] Ordinarily, given the unmanageable numbers of African patients in Weskoppies at that time, officials would have welcomed the possibility of reducing the numbers of those who were neither violent nor dangerous and releasing them to their families' care.[24] But any such desire was checked by the countervailing suspicion that given the tenacity of her delusions, Nontetha may well have been likely once again to prove herself a source of social and political disruption if discharged unconditionally. As Crosthwaite saw it, "Her hallucinations and delusions have never changed in character. They are only less prominent at the moment because she has not an opportunity of feeding them on the credulity and admiration of her followers."

Crosthwaite felt that the matter should be brought before a judicial inquiry for final adjudication. However, he appears to have been overruled by Dunston. Moreover, Dunston, in his capacity as advisor to the Minister of the Interior and as a psychiatrist who had previously examined Nontetha and who "knew Nonteta personally," insisted that should she be released, there would be a repetition of all the "troubles." This decision was relayed to the Native Affairs Department, which in turn communicated with the Aliwal North Native Welfare Society, as well as with family members, informing them that it was necessary still to treat her as mentally unsound. Permission would be given to her followers and relatives to see her. They could also ask for a report from the physician superintendent on her condition from time to time.[25] As a consequence, no further consideration was ever given to Nontetha's release and she would spend the remaining five years of her life within the walls of Weskoppies.

As noted earlier, the purpose of the elaborate procedures of diagnosis at Fort Beaufort and Weskoppies and Nontetha's "labeling" as a sufferer of dementia praecox or paranoia was not to yield understanding or therapeutic benefits for their subject. Indeed, the meticulous classification of patients by disorder—usually for the purposes of gathering statistics for annual reports—rarely held practical implications for the care of African patients. These classifications reveal a great deal more, however, about the protean character of Western psychiatric classificatory systems and their dubious validity.[26] Some writers suggest that the very activity of classification as a discursive practice offered psychiatrists an often illusory sense of having the means to predict, prevent, and control mental disorder, and that the complex classificatory tables made it possible to "create narratives of scientific certainty" at odds with confusion and ambiguity that were endemic to asylum practice.[27]

A Grotesque Crowd of Social Debris

Without the records at our disposal, it is possible to build only a partial picture of Nontetha's ten-and-a-half-year existence at Weskoppies. As noted earlier, despite the meticulous classification of patients according to their disorders, these elaborate conceptual structures and procedures held few practical implications for African patient care. The premium on space precluded the separation of the most disturbed patients in separate wards or facilities, which together with classification, was regarded at the time as an essential precondition for effective treatment. With the exception of the most violent, all patients, regardless of their condition—"catatonic, schizophrenic, dementia praecox etc"—were kept together. And this accounts for the macabre and often disturbing visions that assailed visitors to the hospital. Ralph Bunche was struck by the "grotesque crowd of social debris" that greeted him on his visit to the male "native" yard in 1937. Wulf Sachs, the psychoanalyst and author who worked at the hospital for some of the time during Nontetha's incarceration, described in similar terms the powerful impact of the sight of this yard: "It . . . made a tremendous impression on every newcomer, native or European. The yard consisted of a huge quadrangle, on each side of which was a number of doors. In this quadrangle were about five hundred male patients, of all tribes and ages, talking, shouting, jumping, the brilliant sunshine making grotesque shifting shadows of their antics. Some of the men lay on the ground baking themselves in the hot sun. Near them several human statues seemed to have been posed in fantastic attitudes."[28] Bunche also offers us a rare glimpse of the female "native" section and of Nontetha's fellow inmates: "Unlike the men, many of them talk sex all the time. Several were bold enough to walk around and rub up against us. There are several cases of women who spend their entire days on their knees and with pails of water, scrubbing the floors and walks. One has been doing it for seven years."[29]

Although some African patients' bodies were used for experimental research, on the whole, "treatment" in Weskoppies was confined to "rest." In practice, however, this was difficult to achieve given the space shortages. "Occupational therapy," moreover, meant simply that the sufficiently healthy African inmates were put to menial and cleaning work in the buildings and on the institution's grounds. Mimicking the racial hierarchy and division of labor in the world outside the hospital, African male "working patients" undertook the heaviest manual labor, such as working on septic tanks, in the fields, or in the hospitals' pig sties,[30] while women were set the conventionally "female" tasks of domestic labor in the institution and weeding the grounds. Although white male patients were also used for construction and other maintenance work on the hospital grounds, this racial division of labor is made strikingly clear in the annual hospital reports. Whereas the annual report of 1937 detailed the improvements made to the occupational and entertainment program for white patients, it was noted under the "Natives" subheading, that the "native section of course, are very active and need no additional occupation." Whether Nontetha was considered well enough for this form of "occupational therapy" is not known. If not, she probably spent her days in the wards and yard among the other women.

On the occasions that she was alleged to have attacked other patients, she would have been placed in isolation in accordance with contemporary practice. Perhaps, when "refractory," she was secluded in a refractory ward with its "seething mass of yellow humanity" or else dosed with the potent cocktail of hyoscine, chloral hydrate, and bromide barbiturates that was liberally dispensed to disturbed patients at this time.[31] Given the expense of traveling such a distance, the visits from her family and friends after the 1930 Pilgrimage of Grace tailed off, and thus the consolation and succor she might otherwise have derived from contact with them was only intermittent.

For all the advertised modernity of Weskoppies, contemporary investigations reported appalling living conditions, due primarily to overcrowding. Inmates slept shoulder to shoulder, making up "a solid layer of humanity."[32] Patients without beds slept on mats on the floor, and spilled over into the dining halls and verandas. Staff shortages were acute and regular complaints were made about untrained nurses, the overwhelming majority of whom were white women. Of a nursing staff of 197 in 1934, only 34 were black—8 women to 45 men. Overworked, underpaid, and overwhelmed by the sheer numbers of patients, the trained white nursing staff was most likely to neglect African patients, with whom communication was most difficult. Allegations of abusive treatment of inmates of all racial designations at the hands of staff and warders were common and, in the Weskoppies case, prompted government investigation in 1923. Acknowledging the difficulties in obtaining reliable evidence from mentally disordered patients, the government commission nevertheless concluded that "isolated assaults of a very serious nature" indeed occurred, that unnecessarily harsh handling of patients was a frequent occurrence in the hospital.[33] One former inmate, probably a Coloured man by the name of Baird, complained to the Governor General in May 1929, "It's a disgrace to Christianity the language the staff uses to these patients. I don't think that I'll ever be able to sing or speak right again the way that they strangled me around the neck. I expect that it was because I told them too plainly where they were going if they did not turn unto God."[34]

In the years preceding Nontetha's incarceration, and soon after her death, conditions in mental hospitals came under scrutiny and severe criticism by both the Select Committee of 1913, and later, in 1936, by the committee appointed to investigate conditions in mental hospitals and institutions for the feeble-minded. In his annual report as Commissioner for Mental Hygiene in 1927, Dunston wrote of "grave overcrowding," which resulted in premature discharge of inmates to hopeless surroundings with the attendant danger of their relapsing, falling into "crime of all sorts, illicit liquor selling, diseases, etc." The hospital authorities were clearly overwhelmed by the constant flow of new African inmates, by the incapacity of the institution to cater to them and the anxiety that their very presence compromised the care and treatment of white patients. Anticipating an additional five hundred African inmates within the foreseeable future, the superintendent physician at Weskoppies despaired in 1936 that: "Increasing the natives in this Institution will be detrimental to the treatment and welfare of white patients. The place is already flooded with natives and it makes proper treatment of whites difficult as it affects not only the environment in the Hospital but the attitude of staff and European patients."[35]

The precise reasons for the rapid expansion in numbers of African mental hospital inmates require further research. Without simply accepting the "evils of town" argument, it nevertheless seems plausible that this growth was associated with the social and psychological strains wrought by the hemorrhaging of rural populations, the privations of urban life, and strains placed on existing informal structures of social welfare and healing in both town and country. Those who could not be cared for within rural reserves or locations were increasingly becoming a source of concern for leaders, some of whom saw in mental hospitals a solution to this growing problem. By the 1940s, for example, local African notables of the Pietersburg area of the northern Transvaal communicated their anxieties about the presence of insane Africans repatriated from their areas of urban employment. In 1944 counselors associated with Chief Mphahlele requested the establishment of an asylum in the region.[36] The authorities, however, deemed the numbers of certified insane Africans in that area did not merit the establishment of a local mental hospital, taking comfort from the plans for the construction of the new Sterkfontein Mental Hospital on the West Rand in 1947. With the victory of the National Party in the parliamentary elections the following year on a platform promising "total segregation," or apartheid, yet another phase in the making of a racially skewed mental hospital system was set in place.

5

Dry Bones

The hand of the Lord was upon me, and he brought me
out by the Spirit of the Lord, and set me down in the
midst of the valley; it was full of bones. And he led me
round among them; and behold, there were very many
upon the valley; and lo, they were very dry. And he said
to me, "Son of man, can these bones live?" And I answered, "O Lord God, thou knowest." Again, he said to
me, "Prophesy to these bones, and say to them, O dry
bones, hear the word of the Lord. Thus says the Lord
God to these bones: Behold, I will cause breath to enter
you, and you shall live."

—Ezekiel 37: 1–5

Nontetha told us that she would not return in the same
way she left.

—Comment of a member of the Church of
the Prophetess Nontetha at the exhumation
of Nontetha's grave in Pretoria, July 1998

How can a person be a pauper when they have a family?

—Comment of Notho Guntu at the
exhumation of Nontetha's grave, July 1998

Isolated from all but a few visitors and suffering from a terminal illness, Nontetha must have spent her last years in pain.
Surely she found little relief from anguish in the confines of
Weskoppies. Apart from the peculiarly repressive character of
mental hospitals for black South Africans, it is generally acknowledged that protracted confinement in "total institutions"

such as asylums tends to exacerbate, rather than treat, mental pain. The loss of personal autonomy, the unpredictability of the environment, the coercive practices, and the isolation from a truly therapeutic community are in themselves likely to lead to the kind of depression attributed to Nontetha by the psychiatrists.[1]

On 20 May 1935 Nontetha died of cancer of the liver and stomach at Weskoppies.[2] The superintendent of Weskoppies sent her family a telegram informing them of her death and instructing them to make immediate arrangements for claiming her body in Pretoria. Because communication by telegram to the African reserves was notoriously slow, it was not until 4 June that Reuben Tsoko, one of Nontetha's leading followers, wired a response: "SEND NONTETA DOWN WE WANT TO BURY BY OURSELVES." By then she had already been buried. Citing public health codes, two days after her death officials had wrapped her in a blanket and placed her body in an unmarked pauper's grave at Pretoria's Newclare Cemetery.[3]

Since the miserable state of communications in the rural areas was no secret, it is hard to imagine that hospital officials expected a reply from Nontetha's family or church leaders within two days. When Tsoko did contact them, they resorted to bureaucratic evasions, claiming that the cost of returning her body was too high and that they were prevented from doing so, in any case, by a regulation prohibiting exhumation for a period of two years.[4]

Nontetha's family and followers responded to the news of her death in contrasting ways. One group unsuccessfully pressed for the return of her remains. Shortly after her death, one of her sons, Menzeleleli, traveled to Pretoria to request the return of her body. State officials put him off and showed him a grave where they said she was buried. But Menzeleleli did not accept their explanation because he noted that the grave was overgrown with weeds and therefore too old to be hers. On another occasion a group of her female followers approached the magistrate in King William's Town for the return of her body. His reply was that their request was like a child asking for the sun from the sky. Since officials in Pretoria were responsible for her institutionalization, her followers should contact them.[5]

In 1955 Tsoko, one of the founders of the Church of the Prophetess Nontetha; Dumalisile Bungu, one of Nontetha's sons; Simon Nxepe; and Joseph Zumane contacted the government. This time they repeated their contention that Nontetha had never been mentally ill and demanded that the government open an inquiry into why her rights had been denied and why she had never been released. They expressed their belief that since no prior inquiry had ever been initiated, the government wanted to suppress the matter. Contending that correct procedures had been followed at the time, the government replied that it saw no reason to reopen the case, especially since Nontetha had been dead for two decades.[6] Following this exchange, the leaders of Nontetha's church saw no point in pursuing the case any further, and they never again approached the government.

Another group of Nontetha's faithful, led by her daughter Nontombi, did not accept that Nontetha had actually died in May 1935. Instead they believed that the government was playing a trick on them and had placed her on Robben Island. They remembered Nontetha's statement that she would not be released until all the political prisoners were freed. Thus, when Nelson Mandela and others were let out of prison in 1990, they expected that Nontetha would soon appear. However, when they came to the realization that she was not going to come out, they reluctantly accepted that Nontetha was dead. Before her death in the mid-1990s, Nontombi expressed her hope that one day the remains of her mother would be found and returned to the family home. This was a view shared by all of Nontetha's descendants and church members.[7]

Plot 99

The matter of locating Nontetha's grave was reinitiated in July 1997, when Robert Edgar paid a visit to members of the Church of the Prophetess Nontetha at Thamarha location, near King William's Town. He had met them more than two decades earlier while doing fieldwork on millennial movements in the eastern Cape and Transkei. Although the church had split into three factions, the Thamarha branch claimed 1,000 members, primarily in rural districts stretching from Middledrift to East London. Despite the passage of time, church members remembered Edgar well and welcomed him back warmly. During the course of his conversations with the congregation, he learned that the government's handling of Nontetha's burial and its recalcitrant attitude was still a source of great anguish and anger to her family and church members. Edgar privately resolved to see if her grave could be located, though he wondered whether sixty years later there was even the remotest possibility not only of finding the grave but persuading bureaucrats to assist in arranging for the return of her remains.

However, the elections of April 1994 and the change in government had transformed the political climate for making such inquiries, and there were a few leads from official documents in the State Archives in Pretoria already in hand. For one, it was known that Nontetha died in May 1935 and that she had been buried in "New" Cemetery in Pretoria. After calling all the cemeteries in Pretoria, Edgar could find no cemetery with that name. But talking to Johan Green, supervisor of Rebecca Street Cemetery, he learned that it had previously been known as Newclare Cemetery. Not only did the name fit but the old Newclare was the closest cemetery to Weskoppies where it was possible to bury Africans, albeit in a segregated section. This was a very promising lead.

Fortunately the cemetery had very detailed records of all burials. Therefore, it was a simple matter to ask Green to bring out the oversized burial register for the period when Nontetha died and turn to the pages where burials for May 1935 were recorded. Without too much searching, a handwritten entry for "Nonteto" appeared, dated 22 May 1935. The burial register also noted that she had died in the mental hospital and that she was sixty-two years old, roughly the age we had estimated for her. The only notation in the entry that did not square with the facts we knew was that her sex was listed as "native male."[8]

Paupers were usually buried three deep in a single grave. In Nontetha's case, we learned from the register that there were two bodies in her grave. The day before her burial, the body of Bassop Malambo, an eighty-six-year-old inmate of the Pretoria jail, was buried in plot 99, and Nontetha's body was put on top of his. Had she been buried below the other body, a complex process of securing permission to exhume that body would have been necessary.

The cemetery that became Nontetha's resting place had been located, but the task of pinpointing her grave remained. The register identified plot numbers for each burial, but graves in the pauper's section had no headstones. In fact, in the entire section for Africans in which Nontetha was buried, there is but one row of graves with the headstones of Pretoria notables. One is for William Nkomo, a founder of the ANC Youth League, and another is for Nimrod Tantsi, an AME minister who was chaplain to the ANC for many years. Green showed Edgar a detailed map of every plot in Nontetha's section, and then he escorted him to an area where he pointed to a patch of land. He was confident that this was the place where Nontetha

was buried, and was convinced that once they located reference points, he and his assistants would be able to find the
exact location of her grave.

At this point, Edgar contacted Hilary Sapire to update her
on his discovery at Rebecca Street Cemetery. Since Edgar had
to return to Washington, D.C., and Sapire resides in London,
neither could pursue the matter at first hand. We decided the
best course of action was to gather relevant documents, including a photocopy of the burial register page bearing Nontetha's
name, and have a friend who grew up in King William's Town,
Luyanda ka Msumza, hand carry them to Nontetha's church
and family. When Msumza passed on the documents and information, they caused much excitement. In addition, we contacted officials in the Directorate of Museums and Heritage
Resources of the Eastern Cape provincial government in King
William's Town. Once they learned about Nontetha's story
and her fate in Pretoria, they were intensely interested in pursuing the matter.[9]

The directorate has taken the lead in commemorating the
eastern Cape's past through erecting monuments and in involving local communities in preserving their own histories.
Typically it has tried to link the commemoration of a historical
monument with a development need—so that a community
hall or a health clinic is built in conjunction with the monument. In late 1998 the directorate went a step further by in-
troducing Community Heritage Projects, which provide grants
of R50,000 (about $8,000) to communities to remember local
historical events and important personalities. The projects,
according to a directorate announcement, are aimed at:

providing recognition for neglected sites

redressing imbalances in the portrayal of the history of the
Province

promoting nation building and reconciliation

maximising the tourism benefits of heritage sites

promoting the educational benefit of such sites

The directorate plans to assist local communities with background research, but they have the primary responsibility for initiating a project and deciding on the most effective way—"memorials, cairns, interactive plaques, and commemorative markers"—to carry out their idea.[10]

In subsequent months, close communication was maintained so all parties could be briefed on developments. We made plans to travel to the eastern Cape in March 1998. The trip was scheduled in order to deal with a host of issues related to exhuming the remains and returning them to Nontetha's home. Many questions had to be addressed. Could her plot in Rebecca Street Cemetery really be identified? How could one be absolutely sure that the remains dug up were hers? What is the procedure for exhuming remains? Who would pay for the costs of exhuming and transporting her remains in a casket back to the eastern Cape? Would a ceremony be held to celebrate her return home? How much publicity did her family want and at what stage should media coverage begin?

During the interim, telephone conversations and communications by fax with the provincial government, the family, and members of Nontetha's church were finely tuned, but we were still prepared for last-minute glitches. And, just before we departed Johannesburg for the eastern Cape, one such problem arose when family and church members informed us that they had to attend a funeral on the Sunday that had been scheduled for meetings with us. They graciously changed the date for the meeting to Saturday, and allowed us to meet with them then. Nosabata Morley, Similo Grootboom, and Sitati Gitywa, officials from the Directorate of Museums and Heritage Resources, met us at the homestead of Mzwandile Mabhelu, bishop of one branch of the church, at Thamarha about ten miles west of King William's Town. Despite a warm welcome, it was obvious that a number of sensitive issues had to be addressed. After prayers and hymn singing, the discussions with church elders began. The presence of government officials was useful because they understood what issues needed to be clarified and what lay within their jurisdiction. Mindful of our roles as historians, we knew we were there to serve only as facilitators. All decisions ultimately had to be made by Nontetha's family.

After discussing the main issues with church elders, the group attended a gathering of Nontetha's descendants at Vuyani Bungu's home in an East London suburb. Bungu is a great-grandson of Nontetha, but also a celebrity in his own right. In a country where boxing has gained enormous popularity among blacks, he has been world junior featherweight boxing champion of the International Boxing Federation since 1994. Again, hymn singing and prayer were a prelude to a lengthy round of discussions. First off, we had to tender an apology for initially meeting with the church elders because in matters such as these, the concerns of the family were paramount.

At both the meetings, the two most vexing issues raised concerned responsibility for the various costs and the certainty of confirming that the remains exhumed in Pretoria were actually Nontetha's. Government officials felt that the Eastern Cape government had a moral obligation to assist the process, but wondered what they could pay for in the face of limited resources. They could cover the costs of exhuming Nontetha's remains and pay for a casket, but could not assume the costs of reburial, a gravestone, and a ceremony.[11]

Bones of Contention

How to be absolutely certain that the remains truly belonged to Nontetha was a more contentious issue, due to a highly publicized and embarrassing attempt to recover the skull of the Gcaleka Xhosa chief Hintsa.[12] In 1835, in the midst of a war between the British and Xhosa chiefdoms, the British had lured Hintsa into a trap on the pretense of initiating talks with him. The British threatened to hang Hintsa unless he betrayed other Xhosa leaders. When Hintsa tried to escape, he was shot and killed. A British soldier cut off his ears and mutilated his skull and his body was stuffed in an aardvark hole. Later a popular belief developed among the Xhosa that Hintsa was beheaded and that his skull was spirited back to England. Because Hintsa was not properly buried, it was believed that his spirit roamed the land and was responsible for continuing strife. Returning his skull would bring peace to South Africa. Over the years, the fate of Hintsa's skull had become "a running sore," according to Mda Mda, a lawyer representing the interests of a group of Xhosa chiefs.

In 1992, Chief Nicholas Gcaleka, who claimed to be a descendent of Hintsa, was training to be a sangoma (a healer) when he had a dream in which he was instructed to search for Hintsa's skull. Gcaleka consulted the eminent historian of the Xhosa, Jeff Peires, several years later about Hintsa's fate. Peires informed him that the army division at whose hands Hintsa met his death had been Scottish. However, Peires did not give a ringing endorsement to Gcaleka's mission. He doubted whether Hintsa's skull could be located in a museum and that it could "only be found through inspiration. The trip might be successful . . . as Chief Gcaleka is a traditional healer who depends on inspiration."[13]

Armed with a few leads and the financial backing of several dozen South African companies, Gcaleka and a traveling party of ten set off in early 1996 for Britain in search of Hintsa's skull. Although Gcaleka said his dreams guided him first to the Scottish headquarters of the regiment responsible for Hintsa's death, he soon moved his search elsewhere. In February he found a skull that he claimed was Hintsa's on an estate near Inverness, in Scotland.

The flamboyant Gcaleka's exploits attracted extensive media coverage in South Africa. However, when he returned home with the skull, he was greeted with skepticism by members of the chiefly elite of the eastern Cape and Transkei, as well as members of Contralesa, the ANC-aligned movement of "traditional" leaders, who had been conducting their own investigations during his absence. At their request, Peires sent them a copy of the British Report of the Court of Inquiry of 1835 that indicated that Hintsa's head had been shattered when the Xhosa chief fled from British troops. The report made no mention of Hintsa's head being cut off and taken away as a war trophy. Nicholas Gcaleka was invited to an *imbizo* (assembly) of thirty senior Xhosa chiefs at the great place of Gcaleka Xhosa paramount chief, Xolilizwe Sigcau. They were dubious about Nicholas's claims, especially after reading the 1835 report.

The chiefs confiscated the skull and turned it over to leading scientists, such as paleo-anthropologist Phillip Tobias and forensic geneticist Trefor Jenkins, to conduct tests on its authenticity. Hintsa had been shot behind the left ear, but the skull Nicholas Gcaleka brought back had a hole only on the right side. Moreover, the investigation of Tobias and Jenkins found no evidence of a bullet wound in the cranium and suggested that the hole in the cranium was likely made after the person's death. They concluded that the cranium was that of a middle-aged women of European descent. As Tobias put it, the skull was more likely to be that of a Scottish nanny than Hintsa's.

The Exhumation at Rebecca Street Cemetery

With this fiasco in mind, we knew that we had to confirm that the remains exhumed from Nontetha's grave were really hers. There is an irony in using modern scientific investigative tools to rectify an injustice perpetrated by a previous generation of government psychiatrists who justified their actions with scientific rectitude. Sapire consulted with experienced scientists at medical schools in Pretoria and Johannesburg, who cautioned us about the complexity of this kind of investigation. They pointed out any testing depends on the condition of the skeletal remains that are uncovered. They stressed that family members should be present to validate the credibility of the investigation. Moreover, the scientists had to take great care retrieving all the remains from the grave, cleaning the bones, and taking photographs at every stage of the process.

Then several options existed for examining Nontetha's remains. One was to have a physical anthropologist or a medical specialist examine the bones to determine demographic characteristics—age, sex, cause of death, and racial group—and to see if they matched the facts that we knew about Nontetha. The family would then have to decide whether this was sufficient proof for them.

A longer and more expensive process would have been to conduct DNA testing on the bones. However, such tests depend on the bones not having deteriorated too far to extract sufficient protein. In addition, it would have been necessary to match the DNA with a living descendant. For the most reliable tests, blood samples would have had to be taken from the maternal line in Nontetha's direct family, as this permits access to mitochondrial DNA, which is passed on only through a mother to her offspring and thus is not affected by the mixing of genes from both parents.[14]

We decided to proceed with the first option. After consultations with experts in the field, we asked a team from the University of Pretoria's Department of Anatomy whether they would oversee the exhumation. This department is unusual in having a team of archaeologists attached to it. This step was taken because Maryna Steyn, a professor of anatomy, has research interests in Iron Age skeletal remains. Although her department had undertaken cooperative projects with the university's Department of Archaeology, they wanted to initiate projects of their own that the other department was not interested in pursuing. Therefore, they hired their own archaeologist, Coen Nienaber, in 1995. In South Africa only a professional archaeologist can apply for a permit to excavate sites. Thus, Nienaber had knowledge of the complex procedures for obtaining official permission to exhume a body. He consulted with the Bungu family and Eastern Cape government officials about the host of steps that had to be taken.

Edgar returned to South Africa in early June and consulted with Steyn and Nienaber about when their schedules allowed for an exhumation. Nienaber set 13 and 14 July as possible dates. After consultations with the Bungu family about their availability, we decided to proceed with those dates. We needed a lengthy lead time since it was not clear how long it would take to obtain all the official approvals. First the Bungu family had to send a letter requesting the exhumation. Next the Eastern Cape Department of Health and the eMnqaba community authority (home of the Bungu family) had to approve reinterring Nontetha's remains once they had been exhumed in Pretoria. Then the National Department of Health and Gauteng Province's Department of Health had to approve the exhumation. Finally the office of Gauteng's member of the executive council (MEC) for Development, Planning, and Local Government, which oversees cemeteries, had to add their endorsement.

We also conferred with Johan Green at Rebecca Street Cemetery since he had the task of pinpointing Nontetha's grave. Fortunately he had much more specific information to work with than the researchers who searched for the grave of Enoch Sontonga, composer of "Nkosi Sikelel'i Afrika," several years ago. They knew that Sontonga had been buried in Braamfontein Cemetery in Johannesburg, but there were discrepancies in various publications on the date of his death. Someone located his obituary notice in *Imvo Zabantsundu*, a leading African newspaper, and an entry for an "Enoch" was found in the cemetery register for 1905. It was not uncommon for the surnames of Africans to be omitted in entries. The register also noted a plot number 4885 in the Christian African section. However, in the absence of a detailed map of individual plots, researchers had to rely on an infrared photograph of the cemetery taken in 1970, a shallow dig by archaeologists to identify where paths and graves were in the Christian African section, and a number plate from another grave to locate what they are confident is Sontonga's grave.[15]

In the case of Nontetha's grave, Green not only had a plot number but also a detailed surveyor's map of the "native paupers" section specifying individual plots. He directed surveyors to locate "surveyors pins marking the block of graves from numbers 51–100. The size of the average grave was calculated from the plan and the location of grave 99 was measured from the surveyor's pins set at the north-west corner of grave 51 and the north-east corner of grave number 100. The measurements were checked by measuring to the surveyor's pin set at the south-east corner of grave number 76."[16]

Nienaber took the lead in obtaining permits for the exhumation. However, his task was complicated by adverse publicity generated by another set of exhumations—those of six Umkhonto we Sizwe (MK) cadres hanged in the Pretoria Central Prison in 1964 and 1965 after their convictions for sabotage and conspiracy. Since the apartheid government held that bodies of prisoners still belonged to the state, the MK activists were buried in Pretoria's Mamelodi and Rebecca Street Cemeteries. Their families had long desired to have their bodies returned to a site near the family homes in the Port Elizabeth area. The government agreed to reinter their remains at a Heroes' Memorial and to hold a commemoration service on their behalf on 27 June.

A directive went out to the Pretoria Metropolitan Council to exhume their graves and transport them back to Port Elizabeth in time for the commemoration. However, when relatives, government officials, Truth and Reconciliation Commission officials, and Pretoria City Council officials showed up at Mamelodi cemetery on 22 June to exhume the graves of Daniel Ndongeni, Noali Petse, and Samuel Jonasi, they had not followed the procedures laid down by law. The Metropolitan City Council had not notified the Pretoria City Council that permission had been granted for the exhumations and those conducting the exhumations had not contacted the police, who routinely supervise exhumations. They also had not bothered to consult Willie Matsoko, supervisor of Mamelodi Cemetery, about the location of the graves. After Matsoko objected to the process because regulations were ignored, he went back to his office to identify the precise location of the graves. In his absence, an earth-moving machine went ahead with excavating what was thought were the right graves—with the tragic result that the wrong bodies were exhumed and transported to Port Elizabeth. Embarrassed officials had to rebury the bodies and find the right graves.[17]

Likewise the exhumations of Vuyusile Mini, Sinakile Mkhaba, and Wilson Khanyinge at Rebecca Street Cemetery ended in controversy, as the superintendent was also bypassed and police were called in to halt the exhumations. After heated discussions, the exhumations were allowed to proceed. This time the right graves were opened, but in a crude fashion, so that little care was taken in removing the bodies. Several observers knowledgeable about these operations believe it is likely that a number of bones were left in the mounds of earth piled next to the graves.

For the sake of Nontetha's memory and her family, we resolved that we would not allow a repetition of these incidents when the time came for exhuming her remains. At the same time we realized that Gauteng provincial officials charged with approving exhumations would scrutinize the next request with extra care. A week before the exhumation was due to take place, we still lacked the signature of Gauteng's MEC of Development and Planning, who was out of town that week. By week's end, although the paperwork had reached the MEC's desk and despite promises that a signature was forthcoming the following Monday, we were concerned enough to entertain a proposal to postpone the exhumation for two weeks.

However, too many expectations had been built up in Nontetha's family and church to delay the exhumation any further. After Eastern Cape officials attended a religious service with family and church members on 11 July, a decision was made to leave for Pretoria. On 12 July a government minibus set off on the long journey to Pretoria. Accompanying three government officials were three leaders of Nontetha's church, a granddaughter and two grandsons of Nontetha representing three branches of her family, and ninety-one-year-old Tobi Nokrawuzana, who had been one of the band of pilgrims who had walked for two months to visit Nontetha at Weskoppies Hospital in 1927.[18] This time the journey would take one day, but the minibus followed virtually the same path as the pilgrims had six decades before.

Fortunately the last signature approving the exhumation came the morning of 13 July. Then Nienaber took the last official step—calling the Pretoria police so that a policeman could observe the exhumation. By late morning, family members, church leaders, government officials, the cemetery superintendent, journalists, a playwright, a historian, a policeman, and the archaeologists were at the graveside. Church leaders offered prayers in remembrance of Nontetha's spirit and to thank Jesus for allowing her remains to be exhumed and returned to her home. Referring to biblical scripture, Bishop Mabhelu reminded those in attendance of Jacob, "who died in Egypt" but who "should have been buried in Canaan, the land of his forefathers."[19]

Nienaber's team (Nienaber, Marius Loots, Louisa Hutten, and Erica Labbe) then began the first phase of clearing the grave of a layer of about eighteen inches of topsoil and debris that had accumulated over the years. Then one could clearly see the outlines of a grave framed in ash that had been partly used to fill the grave. Because this area had been a landfill, as earth was removed from the grave, a variety of animal bones and pottery fragments surfaced.

The basic strategy of Nienaber's team was straight out of an archaeology textbook. Because they knew that bodies were buried in Rebecca Street Cemetery with heads facing the west, they estimated where they were likely to find a femur and began carefully digging shallow (six-inch) test pits or trenches with trowels. The femur is a strong bone and less prone to break on contact with a digging tool. If the test pit turned up no evidence of bones, then another layer of earth was removed from the whole grave. Our initial hypothesis was that since the top body buried in a pauper's grave was usually buried about two and a half feet beneath the ground, we expected to find some remains about that depth. However, by day's end, the archaeologists had gone down about three feet with no results.

The next day work resumed at 8 A.M. Nienaber and his colleagues were even more careful with each test pit they dug. When they reached four feet down with no bones surfacing, we did some rechecking with the cemetery register to confirm that there were indeed only two bodies placed in grave 99. We then calculated that since grave diggers typically dug a grave six and a half feet deep it was likely that the two bodies were placed at the lower end of the grave. This meant that Nienaber's team had to dig even deeper before coming across any bones.

Our surmise was correct. Another foot down, fragments of a wooden coffin and iron nails began to appear in the red earth. Then Nienaber found the first evidence of human remains—the imprint of a tibia that had turned to dust. At the other end of the grave, Loots made an even more dramatic discovery—a largely intact skull.

The next day, as Nienaber's team continued the process of uncovering and retrieving the remains, they learned that some of the bones on top had commingled with the bones of the body on the bottom. Nienaber's hypothesis was that since the person on bottom was buried in a coffin, as it disintegrated, the body on top, which was not buried in a coffin, sank even deeper and shared some of the same space with the lower body.

The mood of the onlookers was somber, but among her family members and church leaders, there was a quiet exultation and a confidence that Nontetha's remains had at last been found. Mzimkulu Bungu, who had grown up hearing stories about his grandmother, spoke for all of them: "Now at last we can rest in peace, knowing that we will not die without seeing that our prophet reaches her rightful resting place." Lulangile Leve, an elder in Nontetha's church, echoed him: "Now the people will pray with a peaceful mind, knowing that Nonteta has gone back home."[20]

After Nienaber's team carefully cleaned and wrapped the bones, Nienaber took them to a laboratory at the University of Pretoria Medical School, where he and Steyn examined them in early August. As Nienaber had feared when he and his team were conducting the exhumation, the acidic red clay soil had taken its toll on the bones. They found no ribs, vertebrae, or pelvis, and the hand and foot bones were very fragmentary. However, enough bones survived—especially the skull and mandible and teeth—that Steyn and Nienaber were able to make some important judgments about the sex, age, and height of the person. Even though the pelvis, the usual indicator of sex, was absent, they concluded that characteristics of the skull—its small mastoid processes, a glabella (the ridge between the eyebrows) that was not prominent, and the sharp margins of the superior orbital—proved that the remains were those of a female. They also noted that the cranial sutures were at an advanced stage of closure and that the teeth were so worn that "dentine patches are visible on many of the teeth." These were both indicators that the remains were of a person older than fifty.

Steyn and Nienaber identified two other characteristics that corresponded to things that we knew about Nontetha. They found bony lesions on the skull that indicated the spread of cancer and they estimated that her height was about five feet, six inches. Indeed Nontetha's family remembered that she was taller than average for people in her area.

The cumulative knowledge that we learned as a result of the exhumation has led us to conclude with certainty that the exhumed remains are those of Nontetha. It is highly unlikely that the bones are of anyone else because of a series of linked facts—two skeletons were in the grave, the one on top was a female and the one on the bottom was a male, there was evidence of only one coffin, and the bones were those of an older woman who probably had cancer.[21]

The report of Steyn and Nienaber provided corroborating evidence that Nontetha's remains have been retrieved. However, this scientific evidence is of limited value if it did not square with the spiritual beliefs and cultural logic of her family and church. To them, the circumstances of Nontetha's burial and Edgar's role in locating and assisting with the exhumation of her remains were paralleled in scripture and were a fulfillment of Nontetha's prophecies. Bishop Mabhelu pointed out the similarities of the burials of Jesus Christ and Nontetha. Christ was wrapped in linen after the crucifixion and Nontetha was wrapped in a blanket after her death. Neither was placed in a coffin. Christ was placed in a tomb intended for another man, Joseph of Arimathea, while Nontetha was interred in a grave with a man. Moreover, Edgar played the role of Joseph of Arimathea in taking followers to Nontetha's grave.

Although Edgar thought that he was acting out of curiosity as well as a desire to redress an injustice in searching for her grave, he did not realize that he was also fulfilling a prediction of Nontetha's. When he visited family and church members in mid-August 1998, he was told of Nontetha's words to her followers in the 1920s: "You must look to the Americans. They will help you one day." This statement reflected the influence of a self-styled disciple of Marcus Garvey, Wellington Buthelezi, who had stirred up blacks in the 1920s with his prediction that African-American liberators were coming to South Africa to free blacks from their white oppressors. Nontetha's words were applied to Edgar, whose surprise return in 1997 to visit Nontetha's church was interpreted as a sign that something important was going to happen. They did not anticipate that Edgar was going to search for Nontetha's grave, and he did not inform them that he was going to do it. However, when they received word that he had located her grave, they hearkened back to Nontetha's words. God had anointed this unsuspecting American to carry out this mission.[22]

The Return of Nontetha

Although the story of the return of Nontetha's remains recalled an injustice from a previous era, it resonated with South

Africa's recent political history, where bones and burials have been invested with special meaning. From the 1970s to 1994, funerals of anti-apartheid martyrs often created public spaces for activists to renew resistance against the apartheid regime, serving as vehicles for political mobilization and, some have argued, community healing.[23] During its existence, the Truth and Reconciliation Commission, one of the core institutions charged with the task of national healing, highlighted the iniquities of the apartheid government hit squads by locating the graves of their victims and returning their remains to their families. However, as the public outcries over Sara Bartman (Saartjie Baartman in the colonial record), the Khoisan woman who was displayed in Europe as "the Hottentot Venus,"[24] and the skulls and bones of indigenous South Africans from museums in Britain and South Africa indicate,[25] the highly charged emotion around the fate of human remains is not limited to those who lost their lives in South Africa's recent political history. As Shula Marks has observed, these battles over bones from a longer colonial past represent an attempt to reclaim a dignity and control over the bodies lost to further the causes of colonialism, "progress," and science.[26]

It was within this context that the last chapter of Nontetha's remarkable story took place on 25 October 1998, when her remains were reburied at her home in Khulile village, near Debe Nek in the eastern Cape. The service brought some closure to an injustice that had rankled her family, church, and community for more than six decades. As Lulangile Leve, a church elder, told journalist Maureen Isaacson at the exhumation, the church was "not simply responding to the mood of reconciliation that has swept the country. They have always wanted to rebury their prophet."[27]

In the months after the exhumation, Museums and Heritage Resources officials Mosabata Morley and Sitati Gitywa took the lead in planning the reburial service with Nontetha's family, church, and community. Morley and Gitywa worked tirelessly, shuttling back and forth from Khulile to East London and other places to ensure that all the complex details for the ceremony were worked out—raising money to pay for the occasion and a coffin (the government and the church shared the costs), returning Nontetha's remains from Pretoria, selecting a venue for the service, erecting a headstone and gravesite, arranging for a sound system and chairs, inviting speakers, and arranging a program and preparing a feast for all those who attended.

The University of Pretoria archaeologists—Nienaber, Loots, and Hutten—transported Nontetha's remains in a wooden crate used to store skeletal remains to a funeral parlor at Dimbaza, where a two-hour ceremony was held on 23 October with family and church members in attendance. After her remains were handed over to an undertaker, they were placed in a polished wood casket. The night before the reburial service an all-night vigil was held at Khulile. On 25 October several thousand people attended the funeral, packing a church and spilling over outside.[28] Similo Grootboom presided over a three-hour hymn-filled service at which speeches were made by a family representative, Z. Jadi; Edgar; the director of the Department of Museums and Heritage Resources, Denver Webb; the provincial minister of education, Prof. Mayatula; Nienaber; a representative of the community, Mr. Magwashu; and the bishop of the Church of the Prophetess Nontetha, Mzwandile Mabhelu.

At the conclusion of the ceremony, the mourners filed out of the church and walked in a procession to the gravesite a half-mile away, where a burial service was conducted. The Joe Slovo Secondary School choir led the singing. As the ceremony concluded, Nontetha's casket was lowered into place beneath a new granite headstone. A person in the crowd fired a last salute with his pistol. Only one error—her gravestone recorded the date of her institutionalization in the Fort Beaufort mental hospital as 1918 instead of 1922—marred what had been a moving occasion.

Although Nontetha had died many decades previously, it is difficult not to be moved by the power of her spirit and the impact her story had on a disparate group of people—family, church members, community members, government officials, archaeologists, medical doctors, and historians—who came together to search for, exhume, and return her remains to their rightful place. Because public history events have a way of generating their own momentum, it is not to be doubted that Nontetha's reburial and the telling and retelling of her story will have consequences that we cannot anticipate.[29]

Conclusion

As many historians increasingly tell us, although the mad may have always represented a shadowy and marginal section of a society, their experiences are particularly revealing of broader social concerns. Even if the "madman" is defined as psychotic, write John and Jean Comaroff, "he may nonetheless be the voice of history." The visual imagery and the poetry in the utterances of the mad, they argue, are a forcible reminder that historical consciousness is not confined to one expressive mode.[1] Whether or not Nontetha was mad, her life and words indeed shed light on the many facets of South African history: African Christianity, the importance of gender in religious and social issues, the interconnections between millennial movements and urban political organizations, and the problematic relationship between insanity, resistance, and social control.

Nontetha and the Spread of Christianity in Africa

Nontetha was a minor religious figure who probably would not have come to our attention but for her collision with the state. She operated within a limited area, she attracted a relatively small following, and she never defined her mission in grandiose terms. However, "it is from the local perspective of village and town," as Bengt Sundkler points out, "that a continental profile of church history can be shaped."[2] Because the story of Nontetha reflects just such a local perspective, it provides insights into the incremental ways that religious cultures evolve and illuminates how Africans in the eastern Cape engaged with Christianity.

Scholarship about the spread of Christianity in South Africa has focused on European missionaries and their encounters and discourses with Africans, when an equally fruitful approach is to examine the African encounter with Western Christianity. In the eastern Cape, where Xhosa societies interacted with European missionaries from the early eighteenth century on, Hildegarde Fast has shown how Africans, in the first decades of European missionary activity, were not passive recipients of Christianity. On the contrary, they constantly probed and challenged Christianity on sociological and theological grounds.[3] They commented on what kinds of people converted, how the European missionaries related to British colonizers, and how missionary authority perplexed and challenged African leaders. Africans also questioned how Christianity dealt with the problem of sin, what it had to say about the ancestors and witchcraft, and what it could do to fill the spiritual, health, and material needs of Africans.

A century later Nontetha was grappling with the same questions; she, too, wondered about the relevance and implications of Christianity for her society. She was not inventing anything radically new; rather she was addressing issues that had already been widely debated in the years prior to 1918. It was the crisis generated by the influenza epidemic that lent urgency to her messages and ignited her career as a prophet. Responding to the crisis, she created a theology of comprehension to make sense of the devastation the pandemic had wrought. However, her work also served a wider purpose, and that was to seek an understanding and a way to deal with the profound social, political, and economic changes that were taking place around her. By weaving apocalyptic imagery and prophetic idioms into her prophecies, she explained the immediate crisis of the influenza and addressed the pressing social concerns of the impoverished folk who lived in her area.

Because Nontetha was illiterate, her revelations did not spring from the canon of established mission theology. Instead she had personal visions and drew original interpretations of the Bible "read" from her right hand.[4] Her oral theology drew on a century of indigenous Xhosa Christian experience, represented by figures like the prophet Ntsikana and the independent church leader James Dwane. This served her well because she defined her primary audience as the amaqaba, those who had resisted Western culture. Nevertheless, Nontetha's revelations did validate Christianity, and some of them contained messages advocating the acceptance of certain European ways. Nontetha undertook an important step in spreading Christianity—a step that was being replicated all over Africa; she moved beyond the confines of the established missions and the first wave of independent churches, whose members were generally individuals with some formal education.

Moreover, Nontetha's "public reading of Scripture" allowed her to address the pressing concerns of her listeners at a particular historical moment and "under very culture-specific conditions." Despite urging her followers to become literate in order to read the Bible, her movement—then and now—relied on an "oral" rather than a "literary" text to transmit the word of God through collective prayers, singing, or preaching.[5]

Gender and Religious Movements

As the figure at the center of a prophetic movement, Nontetha takes her place among an impressive circle of African women who took active leadership roles in their churches and communities, rural homesteads, locations, or urban townships immediately after the First World War. Sundkler has suggested that between 1920 and 1960 an unprecedented number of women assumed leadership of established churches throughout Africa. Nontetha, and other examples, provide evidence that women were asserting themselves in independent churches as well.[6] Women were especially drawn to prophetic movements because they provided independent avenues for spiritual initiatives and leadership that were not encouraged in an institutionalized setting dominated by male leadership. In addition, independent churches provided outlets for expressing class and generational relations. In this regard it makes sense that women and schoolchildren were among those most attracted to Nontetha's movement.

The fact that it was a woman, Nontetha, who led a prophetic movement was not in itself unusual because women regularly assumed leadership roles in African religious movements. The unanswered question is, What kind of women assumed these roles? A clue emerges when we recall that before taking up her calling Nontetha suffered symptoms similar to those of ukuthwasa that afflict diviners-to-be. For example, anthropologists have suggested that the role of diviner permits talented and strong-willed women to engage in both a lucrative and socially prestigious profession, in sharp contrast to the generally low status of Nguni women.[7]

An insight into the process through which women in Xhosa societies become diviners, and of the enhanced status this ensured for women, is provided in Nongenile Masithathu Zenani's autobiography (as told to Harold Scheub). As the culmination of her life story, after a detailed account of the rites of passage through marriage and motherhood in which she delineates in painstaking detail the duties and requirements of men and women in the homestead, Zenani tells of her own training as a "doctor" and of the autonomy and independence it conferred upon her. In this process of transition, Zenani briefly left her husband—who had objected to the peripatetic existence required by her professional calling—and set up her own practice. She returned to him only when he became reconciled to her role.[8]

The impression of Nontetha that emerges from both documentary evidence and oral testimony is similarly of such a charismatic and forceful figure. But her authority, credibility, and influence did not derive exclusively from her exceptional personal qualities. As an older woman (in her forties at the time of her prophecies), as a woman who had passed through key rites of passage (marriage, childbirth and rearing, and widowhood), as the head of her own household (there is no evidence of her being subject to the authority of any male kin), Nontetha would have been exempted from some of the restrictions and gender norms to which younger women or married women living in the homesteads of their in-laws were subject. These factors, combined with her already acknowledged position as an herbalist and a seer, prior to her becoming a prophet, would have conferred upon Nontetha a degree of authority and stature that is likely to have ensured her status as a respected prophet.[9] They are also suggestive of the reasons behind the apparent inability and unwillingness of some chiefs and headmen to restrain her when called upon to do so by the state authorities.

In Nontetha's movement, women were especially prominent; and they certainly used this prominence as a vehicle for challenging the established power structure in her area. One of her most loyal supporters and patrons was the wife of the acting chief Ngangelizwe Kama, who was dissatisfied with Tamsanqa Kama's authority. This dissension was a factor in Nontetha's arrest and institutionalization, since the government relied on the cooperation of chiefs and headmen who were upset by Nontetha's activities.

Women were also conspicuous in subsequent campaigns to secure Nontetha's release from the asylums in Fort Beaufort and Pretoria. The mere fact that women were free from pass laws that restricted men's mobility in the Pilgrimages of Grace partly explains why women were as valuable and visible as they were.

Nontetha's position and prominence as a woman also sheds light on the sheer diversity and breadth of female activism in this period. Although the study of gender relations, women's organization, and female activism has advanced in recent years, scholars have generally focused attention on urban women. William Beinart has noted that the relative autonomy women seemed to enjoy in cities allowed them to engage in militant action on issues that were important to them.

Most of the work on rural female resistance has been concerned with the structural conditions of women in rural areas. The abiding image of the rural landscape is the male migrant leaving his wife behind to shoulder the burden of poverty. With some important exceptions, the image has not been accompanied by investigation and analysis of the subjective experiences of rural men and women forced to change the existing pattern of gender relations.[10] At the most general level, this literature reveals that male authority, so fundamental to the culture of African rural societies, persisted and seriously circumscribed the opportunities and scope of female resistance or independent organizational expression.

As Beinart points out, these general analyses of rural immiseration neither fully explain the role of women nor specify the direction of women's political struggle in either the domestic sphere or wider world. And, as Iris Berger adds, these predominantly static accounts fail to address the contradictory evidence of creative and expressive women, of women who enjoyed respected places in the hierarchical orders on which many rural African societies were based, and of women occasionally being able to subvert their subservient roles into forms of power.[11] Few accounts, moreover, offer insights into the significant female involvement in, and support for, prophetic movements and independent churches, phenomena that were considerably more pervasive than much of the literature on either African opposition politics or female activism suggests.

Within that literature, however, there are clues as to why African women in the years after the First World War were attracted to independent church groups. Colin Bundy for one has noted that some women in the East London branch of the Industrial and Commercial Workers' Union (ICU) were viewed as tea makers and social organizers, rather than full-fledged union members. Some of them abandoned the organization for the Wellington movement's combination of radical Africanism and independent Christian rhetoric, and presumably greater space for female expression.[12]

Nontetha's life deepens the inquiry into the particular appeal and meaning of redemptive messages for rural women. Her case also offers a fascinating counterpoint to the better-known aspects of female activism in the urban centers at the time, preoccupied as it was with the more earthly concerns of passes, housing, beer brewing, wages, social welfare, and political representation. While new research will reveal more about how and why urban women experienced enhanced potential for organizational leadership and how power struggles between men and women were played out in the cities, given the predominance of migrancy and the increased tempo of urban immigration during this period, a fuller understanding of social change and gender would be advanced by looking at the rural reserves and the "white" agricultural heartlands. There, in contrast to the cities, it appears that even when female leaders and prophets emerged, the established gender hierarchy was never seriously challenged.[13]

Rural Religious Movements and Urban Political Activism

Because historians have concentrated for so long on urban-based, formal institutional histories of political movements and trade unions, they have only recently explored the interconnections between the ideologies and practices of separatist churches and prophetic movements with the established organizations, such as the ICU or the South African Native National Congress (ANC). Thus, the degree to which the two sets of groups drew upon one another's language, mode of discourse, and method of organization only becomes apparent when one evaluates and compares such work as that of Colin Bundy and William Beinart on the construction of ethnic and nationalist identities in South Africa with the scholarship on formal movements of modernizing nationalist elites.

By the late 1920s and early 1930s, the rhetoric of the African elite melded the political languages of solidarity and trade union unity, black nation building, and freedom with images of fiery prophets, "talking crows," and African-American liberators arriving in airplanes from across the seas.[14] Clifton Crais contends that an examination of this confluence of popular millennial eddies, on the one hand, and the elite Xhosa and African nationalist currents, on the other, illuminates how fundamentally new conceptions of nation, ethnicity, and civic community were being forged in these years.[15]

Although Nontetha and her followers did not define their movement in overt political terms, many of their ideas and the issues they raised overlapped with those of nationalist and trade union movements in nearby East London. As noted above, they all could and did draw from a common pool of traditions, experiences, ideas, and images—for example, Ntsikana and his prophecies, the appeals to chiefs to play a constructive and unifying role in mobilizing Africans, and the expectations of Garveyite liberators.[16]

The symbiotic relationship between prophets and political movements can be illustrated more clearly in the activities of several other women prophets. One was Selina Bungane, a self-proclaimed prophet from Keiskammahoek who started preaching in East London. An ICU member, she spoke at one of their meetings in October 1930, claiming that God had anointed Clements Kadalie as the sole leader of the African people with a special mission to "organize" the Gcaleka Xhosa. Echoes of Nontetha's message crop up in her appeal to her listeners to remember Ntsikana's Day and her warning that "there are some dangerous locusts riding on the ass and they will bite all those people who refuse to accept Kadalie's teaching."[17]

The Zulu prophet Josephina, who hailed from the Ladysmith district in Natal, provides another example of the cultural diffusion that took place. When she appeared on the Witwatersrand in 1923, she shared platforms with speakers from the Transvaal Native Congress, a provincial branch of the ANC. Like Bungane, her message bore many similarities to Nontetha's. Addressing a crowd in the Benoni location on 17 August, 1923, Josephina claimed that God had ordained her to guide people in the correct way of doing things. Like Nontetha, she had begun her prophecies during the 1918 influenza pandemic and she, too, called for people to give up certain practices: "they must unite and . . . they must return everyone to their own native customs; that beer drinks and so-called tea parties must be abolished, whilst native children should not be allowed to play organs, concertinas or guitars, because these led to the children being spoilt."

Citing Deuteronomy 28, she predicted that 1923 would be the year for a plague of locusts and that they would have the heads of human beings and tails like scorpions. She warned that if people ate them they would become ill.[18]

Madness, Resistance, and Psychiatry in South Africa

Nontetha's saga offers a unique window into the world of mental hospitals and psychiatric practices in South Africa during the interwar years. Madness and colonialism as recurring themes in southern African fiction have been acknowledged and studied by students of literature. Similarly, the psychological impact of colonialism, the relationships between anticolonial resistance and insanity, and the function of colonial psychiatry elsewhere in Africa have been dominant concerns in Africanist scholarship.[19] In South African studies, the history of European psychiatry's encounter with Africans and their worldviews, beliefs, and practices, has only recently been addressed by historians and cries out for further research.[20]

One obstacle to writing such a history lies in the paucity of case records. With the notable exception of Valkenberg Hospital, no full case records exist for any institution, and apart from the bowdlerized Weskoppies records, we have not succeeded in locating the detailed case records that are essential to reconstructing the history of mental hospitals and the experiences and voices of their African inmates. The absence of case files from Pretoria Mental Hospital denies us a detailed picture of the daily lives of African inmates within the institution, but thanks to a post-Bulhoek obsession with state security, other state officials have bequeathed a valuable record of the life of one remarkable African woman during her time as a mental patient.

Nontetha's incarceration and the controversy it caused took place at a key moment in the history both of psychiatry and the consolidation of segregationist thought and practice in South Africa in the 1920s and 1930s. Nontetha, both as political subversive and psychiatric inmate, stood at the confluence of events in the 1920s, when the fears unleashed by millennial, Africanist, and nationalist protest movements contributed to the creation of a new, segregationist policy.

The 1920s saw an increase in the number of mental institutions, the professionalization of psychiatry, and its growing influence in fields such as education, social work, and criminology. All this took place in, and contributed to, the making of an increasingly racialized and segregated environment. As Saul Dubow and others have shown, the making of segregationism involved more than the promulgation of exclusivist and discriminatory legislation. To a considerable extent, consolidation of segregationism as a practice was associated with the production of knowledge about "race" that intellectually buttressed the emergent racial order and of white supremacist thought.[21] The nascent specialization of psychiatry was one source of these new reservoirs of knowledge.

Operating in a context of widespread anxiety about "poor whites" and "the future of the race," psychiatrists of this period, together with psychologists, social scientists, and policy makers, shaped policies that privileged the needs of the white insane, deviant, or mentally defective. Thus, while this period saw the identification of "mental deficiency" as a critical problem among whites and the creation of separate institutions, reformatories, schools, and policies to cater to this constituency, the "feeble-minded" African was either not institutionalized, or was left in wards together with a whole range of patients categorized as insane.[22]

Diverse studies on "native mentality" nevertheless contributed to the creation of a body of "scientific" knowledge about the intellectual and emotional difference between white and black, and "proof" of the inferiority of blacks. Complementing a long established social-scientific interest in the workings of the "native mind," South African psychiatric discourse drew eclectically on both older social Darwinist and biological determinist theories of race as well as psychoanalytic theories in a renewed concern to fathom the "native mind." Such theorizing had the effect of conferring authority upon widely held assumptions about the differential cognitive and emotional capacities of black and white. Their writings served to confirm white beliefs that blacks were fundamentally irrational, preoccupied with "witchcraft," and emotionally immature.[23] They also provided a rationale for the inferior and inadequate treatment of black people in mental hospitals.[24]

With respect to colonial Africa, Megan Vaughan has observed that the history of colonial ideas about the "native mind" has only had an indirect bearing on the history of the institutionalization and treatment of the African insane.[25] Similarly, in South Africa the wealth of literature generated in the 1920s, 1930s, and 1940s on African intelligence, or the works of psychoanalytically inclined "ethnopsychiatrists" like B. F. Laubscher, Wulf Sachs, and J. F. Ritchie, did not have an impact on institutional practices or nudge the profession into ameliorating or reconsidering the treatment of African patients in mental hospitals. The research that was conducted into the "native mind" at this time—intelligence testing, for example—was conducted mainly for the purpose of establishing comparisons with white patients. And any policies of reform that resulted from these researches, were directed toward the white wards.[26] Moreover the surgical and other experimentation conducted on African patients in Weskoppies apparently occurred without obtaining the consent of family members, and seems to have been motivated by the satisfaction of scientific curiosity rather than a concern for curing or healing.

The chief influence of the discourse on the "native mind" was the "scientifically proven" assertion of difference between African and white mentality, and of the inferiority of the latter.[27] The Commissioner for Mental Hygiene, J. T. Dunston, and the psychiatrist who authorized Nontetha's long-term incarceration, considered Africans to be "a mentally inferior race."[28]

> . . . in all these generations, the natives have made no progress in any of the arts of civilisation of their own initiative, and that though they have been in closer and closer contact with a white civilisation, their kraal life has been little influenced, it might be inferred that they are mentally an inferior race. Such an impression is further strengthened by many other facts—they are extremely childish and emotional; they lack initiative; they rarely display foresight or worry about the future.[29]

Such scientifically derived theories of difference, together with popular assumptions, determined psychiatric diagnoses and treatment of Africans in mental hospitals. On the one hand, as many writers have observed, the perceived otherness and inferiority of Africans rendered them out of the orbit of "treatment" and therapeutic care. On the other hand, assumptions were made that their "mental inferiority" precluded Africans from experiencing certain sorts of mental disorders. Dunston pointed out that "true paranoia" was unknown among Africans and pondered whether this was because "they have not reasoning power enough to become paranoiacs." [30]

The perceived inferiority of Africans also made it possible

to appropriate their live bodies for experiments that would not have been performed on whites. How else can we account for a series of bizarre "experiments" conducted on African women diagnosed with dementia praecox in late 1926. In the Weskoppies records a box of files titled "Research" contains correspondence between medical officials at Weskoppies and Johannesburg's Non-European Hospital that refers to operations performed on Weskoppies inmates by medical practitioners in the Non-European Hospital. The ovaries of the "Transvaal African baboon" were grafted onto the ovaries of the women in an operation described as "Laparotomy."

It is hardly surprising that the doctors could report no improvement in the women's condition following these surgical procedures, and it is only to be hoped that the mental hospital superintendent did not comply with a further request for "a Male Dementia Pricox [*sic*] patient," on whom Dr. Beyers was "desirous of performing testicular grafts."[31]

The cultural insulation of white psychiatrists from the world of Africans, as well as the contemporary emphasis on the organic etiology of mental disorder, did little to encourage psychiatrists to investigate the social causes of African mental disorder or the cultural idioms through which it was expressed.[32] The language and cultural gulf between patients and psychiatrists meant that psychiatrists relied on the linguistic skills and empathetic bearing of interpreters, often men seconded from the Native Affairs Department.[33] The latter could not always be depended on, and thus diagnoses were compromised all too often. The cumulative effect of these factors was a tendency toward crude stereotyping of patients, according to mental disorder, gender, and race.[34] As late as the 1970s, diagnostic procedures in South African mental hospitals were found to be so inadequate in this regard that the profession came under severe international criticism. Stock diagnoses and a comparative lack of variety in the categorization of

African mental disorder were found to be common throughout the mental health system.

But within even the most bleak and austere of the African wards of South African mental institutions, islands of humanity, compassion, and even community were to be found. There were also concerned voices within the profession that expressed doubt about the capacities of psychiatrists and nurses to understand and care for their African patients. Wulf Sachs, who began "studying Natives" at Weskoppies in 1928, wondered "if it wouldn't be advisable, from a psychological point of view, to employ inyangas in the treatment of insane natives. In any case, there is nothing to lose, for our methods fail lamentably." By contrast, Sachs describes an African warder, N'Komo, whose "handling of the insane was an art in itself," whose "tender, sensitive expression when listening to the difficult, incoherent talk of the patients was often indescribably poignant": "He knew practically every native patient by name, was familiar with his life-history, his past illnesses, and the progress of his mental disease; in fact, his powers of observation and deduction were so developed that the doctors themselves often relied as much on N'Komo as on their own examinations."[35]

While only a minority voice within the profession questioned their efficacy, no one working within the state institutions could deny the massive growth in numbers of Africans. In absolute numbers, however, there never was any "great confinement" in South Africa.[36] In 1919, for example, out of a population of 4.8 million Africans, only 2,135 were institutionalized.[37] Although Africans came to outnumber whites in asylums, the proportion of Africans in institutions to that of the African population as a whole was considerably smaller than that of white mental patients to the white population as a whole. Even though asylums and, later, mental hospitals were primarily places to restrain Africans, it cannot be said that those institutions performed the functions of social regulation or discipline of unruly subaltern classes in the same way that some writers have ascribed to asylums in nineteenth- and twentieth-century Europe.[38] In South Africa, this function was assumed preeminently by the prisons, compounds, and reformatories.[39]

In Nontetha's case, "the asylum" was unquestionably critical in silencing a transgressing and nonconforming African voice. However, incarcerating a politically subversive figure in a mental hospital was an exceptional event, which made sense only within the context of the politically and emotionally charged atmosphere following the Bulhoek massacre. Moreover, while Nontetha's own freedom was circumscribed, her influence continued among her followers, hundreds of miles away.

While the political context explains a great deal, the role of gender in determining Nontetha's fate should not be overlooked. The fact that she was a woman may help explain why a medical rather than a purely custodial solution was sought. It is striking that not one of the many male prophets of the time was institutionalized in a mental hospital. By contrast, when officials wrote about the prophet Josephina, it was to suggest that she was mentally disordered. "There can be no doubt," wrote a police inspector, "that 'Josephina' is not mentally normal as she keeps on repeating the same phrases over and over."[40]

The considerable literature dealing with "female madness" in other national contexts is only of limited utility in accounting for Nontetha's route to "the asylum." With particular reference to nineteenth-century Britain, historians have demonstrated that women who deviated from the prescribed attributes of female comportment—subordination, demureness, and sexual restraint—were vulnerable to the possibility of being placed under psychiatric restraint. Traits deemed acceptable in men, such as self-reliance, sexual experimentation, or intellectual

aspirations could be interpreted as evidence of mental disturbance in women.[41]

But in South Africa in the 1920s, although there is clear
evidence of mental hospitals and reformatories playing similar roles in ensuring conformity with prescribed gender roles
among white women, for African women the pattern was quite
different. Throughout the country, but especially in the rural
areas, the central state authorities left it up to African male
patriarchs to ensure female compliance with prevalent gender
"norms." In a whole range of sensitive issues, such as African
sexuality and marriage, white officials were well aware that
when it came to "their" women, "African men were often fiercest
in redefining their personal authority and the integrity of 'customary ways.'"[42] Conversely, "loose" or "unattached" African
women, who were apparently free from African male authority figures, whether they were fathers or husbands, were universally regarded as the scourge of the towns, the source of
moral depravity, and the root cause of the dreaded "detribal-
ization." Such women were stigmatized not only as lascivious
and immoral, but as a source of danger to the broader society.[43] The apparent failure or unwillingness of men to restrain
Nontetha from preaching, and indeed, the fact that some of
her staunchest supporters were male adults, forced the state
authorities to usurp African men's functions in maintaining
authority and to take drastic action. This they did in late 1922,
when she was arrested for the first time.

It seems that it was only when she was in prison, awaiting
her trial, that the police and juridical authorities suspected that
Nontetha was "mad," rather than using religiosity as a blind
for subversive political acts. And it was at this moment, therefore, that the psychiatric institutions became implicated in the
state efforts to silence her. Labeling Nontetha as mad offered
a convenient justification for the most zealous of state authorities for coercive actions against her and a means of preempt-

ing criticism from those quarters seeking to placate African communities, particularly African men, in this volatile period. The committal of Nontetha to a mental hospital was thus an attractive option: It removed a persistently troublesome leader from her followers. At the same time, the imprimatur of expert psychiatric opinion, combining the authority of "science" and the humanitarian gloss of "medicine," meant that such a decision could be represented in humanitarian rather than custodial terms.[44] Moreover, as we have pointed out, it was hoped that labeling Nontetha as mad would discredit her movement. The authorities probably believed that Nontetha would disappear into obscurity in the isolated Fort Beaufort Hospital with its predominantly chronic and incurable cases and low public profile.

Nontetha was not the typical asylum inmate. Her initial incarceration was motivated on political grounds, with the intention of dealing her movement a death blow. When it became apparent that African male figures of authority were unwilling or unable to restrain her from preaching, drastic action on the part of state officials became imperative. This action was taken in late 1922, when Nontetha was first arrested.

We do not have access to records that demonstrate precisely how the decision was made to "pathologize" Nontetha as mad. We do know that prior to her arrest, in late 1923, the authorities suspected her of being a "normal" subversive, troublesome leader who was using a screen of religiosity to mask her political aspirations. Neither did any of the local headmen who opposed her presence or African policemen describe her as mad.[45] It would appear that only after she was arrested was the decision taken to have her examined by medical doctors to determine whether she was "of sound mind." Possibly, upon her arrest, it would have become evident to the authorities that Nontetha was indeed totally sincere about her prophetic role, and this, in the eyes of the authorities would have indicated that she was not in her right mind. We might speculate, too, that the possibilities of permanently removing her through incarceration in a mental hospital and thereby stigmatizing her was a more promising and less controversial means of silencing her than confinement in prison.

Once Nontetha had been declared to be "of unsound mind" and therefore unfit to stand trial, the psychiatric institutions and professionals had become inextricably involved in the government authorities' endeavors to silence her. For the most zealous officials seeking to deal with the Nontetha phenomenon, labeling her as mad conveniently justified coercive action against her—such as being forcibly carried off by police and transported to the Fort Beaufort asylum on her second committal there—as well as her long-term incarceration.

However, if there were differences of opinion between various state actors regarding the incarceration and subsequent release of Nontetha, neither was there any simple collusion between the various state and psychiatric authorities. The complex relationship that would ensue between the state and psychiatric authorities was heralded in the local magistrate's rebuke to the Fort Beaufort superintendent for releasing Nontetha in January 1923 without consulting with him. However, when faced with petitions for her release in 1927, the Secretary for Native Affairs was scrupulous in his insistence that "the matter be determined solely with reference to her mental condition as certified by the proper [psychiatric] authorities."[46] Moreover, there was some difference of opinion within the ranks of the psychiatrists over the diagnoses made, and over the desirability of her continued institutionalization. However influenced they may have been by the publicity surrounding the case, the psychiatrists who examined Nontetha in 1930 were painstaking in supplying expert professional diagnoses of her mental state and in furnishing "sound" medical grounds to authorize her incarceration. In doing so, they were also demonstrating their professional independence and integrity. The quasi-theatrical and ritualistic quality of the procedures and consultation with the authorities emphasized their role as repositories of specialist knowledge of the human mind. As Sally Swartz has observed, at this time psychiatrists were concerned to enhance their influence both within the medical profession and in society at large.[47] It is ironic that it was because of the political urgency of her case, standing at a moment of psychiatry's growing concern to demonstrate its worth, that Nontetha was lavished with a rare level of diagnostic scrutiny in the otherwise grim anonymity of South Africa's mental hospitals. Tragically for her, this concentration of psychiatrists' energy and knowledge only served to confirm the government's verdict that her personal freedom constituted a threat to the social order.

Appendix

Document 1

*Secretary for the Interior, Union Buildings, Pretoria,
to Secretary for Native Affairs, 16 May 1928**

With reference to your communication No. N.A. 11/328 of the 8th instant, regarding mental patient Native female Nonteta. I have to inform you that this case was specially referred to Dr. Dunston, the Commissioner for Mental Hygiene, who himself made a careful examination of the patient. Dr. Dunston is satisfied, as a result of this examination, that it is undesirable that Nonteta should be released under any circumstances. He feels that where-ever she goes she will create a disturbance and cause trouble. He reports that visits from her relatives and followers have a very disturbing influence and make her mentally worse, and for that reason he has forbidden them to visit her.

I should be glad to learn whether you could make this known among her followers in order to save them the trouble of coming to Pretoria and then being unable to see the patient.

*These documents are found in the State Archives, Pretoria, BAO 6605 11/328.

Document 2

F. D. Crosthwaite, Physician Superintendent,
Office of the Mental Hospital, Pretoria,
to J. Dunston, Commissioner for Mental Hygiene,
Pretoria, 2 June 1930

With reference to the detention at this Hospital of Female Native patient Nontete, No. 859, I have the honour to report as follows:-

At a conference held at this Hospital on May 1st, 1930, Nontete was seen by all the medical staff, who were unanimous in the opinion that the patient was mentally disordered and properly detained in the Mental Hospital on the grounds that the following symptoms have been repeatedly and constantly observed during her detention here:-

1. Acute hallucinosis.

2. Delusions of a grandiose nature.

3. Delusions of poisoning.

4. Emotional attitude of religious exaltation with a state of restless excitement.

History and Description of Case.

The patient is aged 58 as nearly as can be ascertained. Her physical appearance is consistent with the stated age. She was first admitted to the Fort Beaufort Mental Hospital on the 9th December, 1922. According to the case records whilst at Fort Beaufort she was in a state of religious exaltation, stating that she was directly inspired by God who, himself, appears to her if she makes certain signs. God then enters her blood and puts writing into her head which she can read and understand. God tells her she must preach.

On January 5th, 1923, she was discharged on three months

probationary leave, but on April 8th, 1924, the Magistrate, King William's Town, reported that she was a source of trouble as <u>she spent all her time preaching to the Natives</u> [underlined in original]. In consequence of this report she was returned to the hospital when it was found that her mental condition was much the same the same as at the commencement of her probationary leave. She stated that she was inspired directly by God, that she had to obey him and preach if he told her to do so. God had picked her to preach to the natives because all their sins would rest on her if she did not.

It therefore appears that from the date of her admission her religious exaltation has been accompanied by an acute and constant hallucinosis.

Whilst at Fort Beaufort she is described as standing and preaching over the fence to nobody in particular, or praying over patients. She is described as looking into her hands and reading messages that she says are visible to her there. Sometimes she preaches with great vehemence and fervour and shows a militancy in her religious practices. On one occasion, whilst detained at Fort Beaufort, she became so noisy and hostile that she had to be isolated in a special airing garden.

At Fort Beaufort is first noticed the presence of a particular delusion, which takes the form of accusing the doctor of having in his possession a letter which belongs to her. The letter which she accuses the doctor of wrongfully detaining, she asserts comes from England and is addressed to her by the father of Queen Victoria. Until this letter is given to her she will continue preaching and singing.

At Fort Beaufort, also, is first noticed the appearance of delusions of poisoning for she accused the staff of giving her poison in her drink.

On December 4th, 1924 she is noted as saying that Queen Victoria speaks to her and tells her that everything she, Nontete, says is true.

Whilst here in Pretoria the same phenomena have been repeatedly and constantly observed.-

Religious exaltation.

Restless excitement.

Acute hallucinosis.

Delusions of grandiose nature.

Delusions of poisoning.

In addition she says that her body is burnt with fire night and day and that this fire is conveyed to her body by the doctors present at this Conference. She asserts that she is a Prophetess directly inspired by God. She also repeats that the doctor has a letter belonging to her from Queen Victoria.

At times she is violent and aggressive and has attacked other patients for no reason, apart from her disordered promptings.

During the past year or so she has become much less vehement and much less militant and for a considerable period of time has shown no aggressive violence. All members of the Conference are agreed that she is mentally disordered and not merely a fanatic. She is undoubtedly the subject of aural, visual and sensory hallucinosis.

Although in 1922, a diagnosis of Praecox, sub-group Hebephrenia, was made, prolonged observation has shown Mannerisms, Psychic Ataxia with senseless incomprehensible conduct to be conspicuous by their absence. Neither have sharp changes of mood been specially noticed. The emotions would appear to correspond to the ideas, and the states of mild depression that have been occasionally observed are, in my opinion to be ascribed to the thwarted desire for release or may perhaps be only apparent as the result of temporary defervescence of the religious exaltation. The delusional content and field of hallucinosis would appear to be stable and coherent and not the reverse, and, on the whole, I am of opinion that she is probably properly to be placed, as regards diagnosis, amongst the Paranoiacs, sub-group "Prophets, Saints and Mystics" amongst whom visionary experiences are common.

Prognosis.

The presently observed modifications in the conduct and behaviour of the patient in the direction of less aggressiveness, cessation of hostile violence, diminution of fanatical and religious zeal, and, generally speaking, of a dying down of the mental, emotional and physical activities, are, in my opinion, to be ascribed to the gradual onset of senility.

It is not to be expected that the delusional beliefs will continue to be held, however, less tenaciously, and a regaining of insight is not to be looked for; so long as mental activities are possible for her; so long will Nontete remain convinced that she is a directly inspired prophetess of God with a message for her own people, which none but she can deliver.

The following questions may arise and I have endeavoured to answer them:-

1. Is there any reason why Nontete should not be allowed conditional discharge to specified relatives?

Nontete is not a danger to herself, and there is no reason why she should not be so discharged having regard only to her mental condition.

2. Is Nontete likely to again prove herself a source of disturbance, and possibly, danger to the preservation of order amongst her people, if discharged conditionally?

The answer to this question must be "yes." Not much encouragement would be needed I fancy to rekindle her activities in the direction of her mission, and it is very difficult to estimate the probable strength of the restraining influence exercised by her knowledge of what would happen if she broke the conditions of discharge.

3. Is it advisable to refuse a conditional discharge and to bring the matter to the length of a Judicial Enquiry?

Yes.

Document 3

Dr. J. Dunston, Commissioner for Mental Hygiene, Pretoria,
to J. F. Herbst, Department of Native Affairs,
Pretoria, 11 June 1930

With reference to your semi-official letter of the 18th March last addressed to Dr. Mitchell in regard to the case of Native female mental patient Nontete, and enclosing a letter from the Honorary Secretary to the Aliwal North Welfare Society, I forward herewith a copy of a report by the Physician Superintendent of the Pretoria Mental Hospital. You will see that he answers the essential questions in the last paragraph of his Minute and although he does not regard Nontete as a danger to herself he is satisfied that she is likely again to prove herself a source of disturbance and possibly a danger to the preservation of order amongst her people.

I would add that I know Nontete personally and well acquainted with her case and I would express my opinion much more strongly than Dr. Crosthwaite has. I feel sure that if she is discharged there will be a repetition of all the troubles which occurred before she was sent to Mental Hospital. Her hallucinations and delusions have never changed in character. They are only less prominent at the moment because she has not an opportunity of feeding them on the credulity and admiration of her followers.

With regard to the letter addressed, I presume, to Mr. Sephton by Mr. Charles Crabtree, I would make the following remarks in regard to –

(2) Expert medical advice has been taken and it has been found necessary still to treat Nontete as mentally unsound.

(5) The deputation mentioned has already been allowed.

(6) The relatives of Nontete can write at any time to the Physician Superintendent of the Pretoria Mental Hospital for a report on her progress.

Notes

Foreword

1. Megan Vaughan, *Curing Their Ills: Colonial Power and African Illness* (Cambridge: Polity Press, 1991), 102.

2. Jonathan Sadowsky, *Imperial Bedlam: Institutions of Madness in Colonial Southwest Nigeria* (Berkeley: University of California Press, 1999), 5; Sally Swartz, "Colonialism and the Production of Psychiatric Knowledge at the Cape, 1891–1920" (Ph.D. dissertation: University of Cape Town, 1996), 7.

3. Vaughan, *Curing Their Ills*, 101.

4. Sadowsky, *Imperial Bedlam*, 149.

5. Roy Porter, *A Social History of Madness: Stories of the Insane* (London: George Weidenfield and Nicholson, 1987), 2.

Introduction

1. Hannah Arendt, *Eichmann in Jerusalem: A Report on the Banality of Evil* (New York: Viking, 1963), 232–33.

2. Shula Marks, "Rewriting South African History; or, the Hunt for Hintsa's Head," Seventh Annual Bindoff Lecture, Queen Mary and Westfield College, University of London, 12 March 1996, 3. See also Sarah Nuttall and Carli Coetzee, eds., *Negotiating the Past: The Making of Memory in South Africa* (Cape Town: Oxford University Press, 1998).

3. We are grateful to Rob Turrell and Shula Marks for their observations on the rich potential of "microhistory" in illuminating the

intimate connections between the personal, political, and psychological in southern African historical studies. See Shula Marks, ed., *'Not Either an Experimental Doll': The Separate Worlds of Three South Africa Women* (London: Women's Press, 1987); Shula Marks, "'Not Either an Experimental Doll': The Separate Worlds of Three South African Women: Ten Years On," paper presented to the Gender in Empire and Commonwealth, Societies of Southern Africa joint seminar, Institute of Commonwealth Studies, London, 16 October 1997; Robert Turrell, "Hanging Women: The 'Singular Case' of Mietje Bontnaal," paper presented to the Societies of Southern Africa seminar, Institute of Commonwealth Studies, London, 25 April 1998, 1–2.

4. At the time of writing, South Africa's mental hospitals and mental health systems have attracted widespread media attention. While one submission to the Truth and Reconciliation Commission alleged that psychiatrists and psychologists were complicit in the violation of human rights under apartheid, the national government's plans to release thousands of psychiatric patients into the care of their families and primary health care institutions have been at the center of controversy. Opponents of this program have pointed to the costs and problems of deinstitutionalization in the United States and the United Kingdom. See "Horrors of Mental Camps before Truth Body," *Weekly Mail and Guardian*, 20 June 1996; "Thousands to Leave Mental Homes," *Weekly Mail and Guardian*, 9 May 1997; "Shutting Another Door on the Mentally Ill," *Weekly Mail and Guardian*, 28 November 1997; "South African Health in Need of Treatment," *Weekly Mail and Guardian*, 22 May 1998.

5. Ann Stoler and Frederick Cooper, eds. *Tensions of Empire: Colonial Cultures in a Bourgeois World* (Berkeley: University of California Press, 1997), vii–viii (as cited in Marks, "'Not Either an Experimental Doll'").

6. Robert Edgar, ed., *An African American in South Africa: The Travel Notes of Ralph J. Bunche*, (Athens: Ohio University Press, 1992), 188–89.

7. Roy Porter, *Mind-Forg'd Manacles: A History of Madness in England from the Restoration to the Regency* (London: Athlone Press, 1987), 5.

Chapter 1

1. Oral testimony from her family and acquaintances relate that Nontetha was born after a major flood of the Buffalo River and before the War of Ngcayecibi (1878–79). This date corresponds with the estimates of hospital officials of her age when she was committed to the mental asylum in Pretoria.

The imiDushane are a subbranch of the Ndlambe Xhosa. Dushane was a Ndlambe military leader who figured in the battle of Amalinde in 1818, when Ndlambe forces trounced Ngqika forces decisively. For his leadership abilities, he was elected commander-in-chief of the Ndlambe army.

2. This transformation is discussed in Colin Bundy, *The Rise and Fall of the South African Peasantry* (Berkeley: University of California Press, 1979) and Les Switzer, *Power and Resistance in an African Society: The Ciskei Xhosa and the Making of South Africa* (Madison: University of Wisconsin Press, 1993).

3. See Cherryl Walker, "Gender and the Development of the Migrant Labour System c. 1850–1930," in *Women and Gender in Southern Africa to 1945*, ed. Cherryl Walker (London: James Currey, 1990), 168–97.

4. For discussions of the division between red people and school people, see Philip Mayer with Iona Mayer, *Townsmen or Tribesmen: Conservatism and the Process of Urbanization in a South African City* (Cape Town: Oxford University Press, 1961) and Philip Mayer, "The Origin and Decline of Two Rural Resistance Ideologies," in *Black Villagers in an Industrial Society: Anthropological Perspectives on Labour Migration in South Africa*, ed. Philip Mayer (Cape Town: Oxford University Press, 1980), 1–80.

5. Monica Hunter Wilson and Leonard Thompson, eds., *Oxford History of South Africa*, 2 vols., vol. 2, South Africa, 1870–1966 (Oxford: Oxford University Press, 1971), 75. William Beinart and Colin Bundy, however, assert that communities in the King William's Town district had not been very receptive to the modernizing political initiatives led by mission-educated "new men" at the turn of the century. See William Beinart and Colin Bundy, *Hidden Struggles in Rural South Africa: Politics and Popular Movements in the Transkei and Eastern Cape, 1890–1930* (Johannesburg: Ravan Press, 1987), 309.

6. Interview, Nontombi Bungu, daughter of Nontetha, Ndindwa location, Middledrift, 1 June 1974.

7. Interview, Reuben Tsoko, Ndindwa location, 31 May 1974.

8. See W. D. Hammond-Tooke, *Rituals and Medicines: Indigenous Healing in South Africa* (Johannesburg: Ad. Donker, 1989), 105–6. See also Monica Hunter Wilson, *Reaction to Conquest: Effects of Contact with Europeans on the Pondo of South Africa*. 2d ed. (London: Oxford University Press, 1961), chapter 7; B. A. Pauw, "Universalism and Particularism in the Beliefs of Xhosa-speaking Christians," in *Religion and Social Change in Southern Africa*, ed. Michael Whisson and Martin West (Cape Town: David Philip, 1975), 153–63. For a discussion of the enduring—and changing—influence of herbalists in an urban context in twentieth-century South Africa, see R. P. A. Dauskardt, "The Evolution of Health Systems in a Developing World Metropolis: Urban Herbalism on the Witwatersrand" (M.A. thesis, University of the Witwatersrand, 1994).

9. See John H. Soga, *The Ama-Xosa: Life and Customs* (Lovedale: Lovedale Press, 1931).

10. What was critical, however, was that the diagnosis involved a consensus between the voices of the ancestors spoken through the igqira on the one hand, and the therapy group on the other.

11. Soga, *Ama-Xosa*, 160.

12. Hammond-Tooke, *Rituals and Medicines*, 108.

13. Soga, *Ama-Xosa*, 155–82.

14. B. J. F. Laubscher, *Sex, Custom and Psychopathology: A Study of South African Pagan Natives* (London: Routledge, 1937), chapters 3 and 11. See also Jock McCulloch, *Colonial Psychiatry and "the African Mind"* (Cambridge: Cambridge University Press, 1995), 49. The nature and function of ukuthwasa has been much debated by psychologists and anthropologists. In the 1970s, many writers, notably Jungian and phenomenological psychologists, spilled much ink in disputing the view that ukuthwasa is due to a mild form of schizophrenia. Nevertheless, the anthropologists David Hammond-Tooke and Manton Hirst argue that there indeed is a psychological dimension to the condition. As Hirst explains, such individuals who would have experienced this calling are likely to be sensitive, perhaps "slightly neurotic." Personal communication to Hilary Sapire, March 1998; Hammond-Tooke, *Rituals and Medicine*, 116; and Steven Feier-

man and John Janzen, eds., *The Social Basis of Health and Healing in Africa* (Berkeley: University of California Press, 1992), introduction.

15. Feierman and Janzen, *Health and Healing in Africa*, introduction.

16. Howard Phillips, *"Black October": The Impact of the Spanish Influenza Epidemic of 1918 on South Africa*, Archives Year Book for South African History (Pretoria: Government Printer, 1990). For examples of how the pandemic affected religious movements in southern Africa, see T. O. Ranger, "Plagues of Beasts and Men: Prophetic Responses to Epidemic in Eastern and Southern Africa," in *Epidemics and Ideas: Essays on the Historical Perception of Pestilence*, ed. T. O. Ranger and Paul Slack (Cambridge: Cambridge University Press, 1992), 241–68; Ranger, "The Influenza Pandemic in Southern Rhodesia: A Crisis of Comprehension," in *Imperial Medicine and Indigenous Societies*, ed. David A. Arnold (New York: St. Martin's, 1989), 172–89.

17. Howard Phillips, *"Black October,"* 162.

18. Ibid., 237.

19. Ibid., 81.

20. See the testimony of Rev. Walter Rubusana, a well-known East London clergyman and politician; James Henderson, the principal of Lovedale Institution; and John O'Donnell, the magistrate of King William's Town, in East London on 7 January 1919 (Union of South Africa, *Commission on the Influenza Epidemic: Evidence 1918– 1919*).

21. Our recounting of Nontetha's illness and dream are derived from a written statement provided by Dumalisile Bungu, a son of Nontetha, in May 1974 and two written accounts, *Isiprofeto sika Nontetha* [Prophecy of Nontetha] and *Inteto ze Sipolofitesho* [Sayings of Prophecy], provided by the Church of the Prophetess Nontetha in July 1997.

22. Interview, Jongile Peter, Ndindwa location, 1 June 1974.

23. Bengt Sundkler notes that dreams and vestments are often linked in the conversion experiences of other African religious leaders. See Bengt Sundkler, *The Christian Ministry in Africa* (Uppsala: Swedish Institute of Missionary Research, 1960), 25–31.

24. In his study of urban prophets in Soweto, Martin West has also observed the similarities between diviners and prophets, many of whom are women. West notes that most prophets have a history

of illness that has been cured by another prophet. See Martin West, *Bishops and Prophets in a Black City: African Independent Churches in Soweto, Johannesburg* (Cape Town: David Philip, 1975), 99–104; and Bengt Sundkler, *Bantu Prophets in South Africa*, 2d ed. (London: Oxford University Press, 1961), 184–86. To diviners, rivers also have been symbolic metaphors for ancestors. See Manton Hirst, "A River of Metaphors: Interpreting the Xhosa Diviner's Myth," in *Culture and the Commonplace: Anthropological Essays in Honour of David Hammond-Tooke*, ed. Patrick McAllister (Johannesburg: Witwatersrand University Press, 1997), 217–50.

25. We thank Manton Hirst for interpreting this reference.

26. See Maurice Bloch and Jonathan Parry, "Introduction: Death and the Regeneration of Life," in *Death and the Regeneration of Life*, ed. Maurice Bloch and Jonathan Parry (Cambridge: Cambridge University Press, 1982), 1–44.

27. Nontetha's prohibitions paralleled those of another prophet, Magaqana, who began holding revival meetings among Ndlambe and Rharhabe Xhosa around the Stutterheim area about the same time. Claiming that he had died and risen with God-given instructions to preach, he attacked witchcraft, excessive drinking, and the dance that took place before the male circumcision ceremony. However, he maintained that because Christ had been circumcised, circumcision itself was acceptable. He stressed observing the Ten Commandments and called for African unity. He told his followers to wear Western clothing because it was acceptable in the eyes of God. Although he enjoined his followers not to leave their own churches, he never attempted to establish his own church. He prophesied that a day of judgment was drawing nigh in which Christ would appear in the sky and judge the righteous and unrighteous. Interview, A. M. S. Sityana, Fort Hare University, 13 June 1974.

28. In the 1950s younger members of Nontetha's church began questioning the need to refrain from shaking hands and began to do it in private. As a result, the church abandoned the prohibition around that time.

29. Interview, Jongile Peter.

30. The mountain was named after the Khoi chief Ndoda, who was killed in battle with the Xhosa chief Rharhabe in the late eighteenth century.

31. For a discussion of Ntaba kaNdoda's significance, see Janet Hodgson, "Ntsikana, History and Symbol: Studies in a Process of Religious Change among Xhosa-Speaking People," (Ph.D. dissertation, University of Cape Town, 1985), 316–19.

32. J. B. Peires, *The House of Phalo: A History of the Xhosa People in the Days of Their Independence* (Johannesburg: Ravan Press, 1981); Peires, *The Dead Will Arise: Nongqawuse and the Great Xhosa Cattle-Killing Movement of 1856–57* (Bloomington: Indiana University Press, 1989); Clifton Crais, *White Supremacy and Black Resistance in Pre-Industrial South Africa* (Cambridge: Cambridge University Press, 1992).

33. C. Brownlee to J. Maclean, 11 May 1856, 60–61, Cape Archives, British Kaffraria (BK) 70, Gaika Commissioner, 1853–1856. We thank Jeff Peires for this reference.

34. Hodgson, "Ntsikana," 222.

35. Ibid., 163–65.

36. This point about Nontetha is also made in Clifton Crais, "Representation and the Politics of Identity in South Africa: An Eastern Cape Example," *International Journal of African Historical Studies* 25.1 (1992): 115.

37. Hodgson, "Ntsikana."

38. On Dwane, see S. M. Burns-Ncamashe, "An Investigation into the Provision of Education of the Order of Ethiopia to Africans in the Cape Province between 1900 and 1952" (B.Ed. thesis, University of Cape Town, 1954); James Campbell, *Songs of Zion: The African Methodist Episcopal Church in the United States and South Africa* (New York: Oxford University Press, 1995), 216–22.

39. Interview, Nontombi Bungu.

40. We are grateful to Deborah Gaitskell for drawing this to our attention. See a series of articles by Gaitskell on African women and Christianity: "Devout Domesticity? A Century of African Women's Christianity in South Africa," in *Women and Gender in Southern Africa to 1945*, ed. Cherryl Walker (London: James Currey, 1990), 251–72; "Power in Prayer and Service: Women's Christian Organizations," in *Christianity in South Africa: A Political, Social, and Cultural History*, ed. Richard Elphick and Rodney Davenport (Berkeley: University of California Press, 1997), 253–67; and "Praying and Preaching: The Distinctive Spirituality of African Women's Church Organizations,"

in *Missions and Christianity in South African History,* ed. Henry Bredekamp and Robert Ross (Johannesburg: Witwatersrand University Press, 1995), 211–32.

41. Ntsikana composed four hymns in his lifetime that have become standards in the Xhosa hymnbooks of several denominations. For a discussion of these hymns see Janet Hodgson, *Ntsikana's "Great Hymn": A Xhosa Expression of Christianity in the Early Nineteenth Century Eastern Cape* (Rondebosch: Centre for African Studies, University of Cape Town, 1980).

42. Ntsikana read his teachings, prophecies, and hymns from the hem of his cloak. Hodgson, "Ntsikana," 157.

43. Interview, Jongile Peter. Nontetha's advocacy of mission schooling was similar to that of the Liberian-born prophet William Wade Harris, who evangelized in Côte d'Ivoire around the First World War. He instructed his followers to attend schools so that they could read the word of God. See Sheila Walker, *The Religious Revolution in the Ivory Coast: The Prophet Harris and the Harrist Church* (Chapel Hill: University of North Carolina Press, 1983), 43.

44. Commanding Officer, South African Police, King William's Town, 19 August 1923, State Archives, Pretoria, Justice Department (JD) 276, file 2/950/19.

45. The umnqayi was also presented to initiates at circumcision schools and was blackened in an initiation fire. The umnqayi symbolized the initiates' new status as Xhosa men and was carried when they attended to any business with legal ramifications or when they consulted diviners and herbalists. The stick that married women carried was their husband's. Philip Mayer, *Socialization: The Approach from Social Anthropology* (New York: Tavistock, 1970), 165. We thank Manton Hirst for this reference and for explaining the umnqayi's significance for women.

According to Gerhardus Oosthuizen, Zulu Zionist prophets commonly wear belts or cords and carry staves because they believe, among other things, that they can protect believers against evil forces. Gerhardus Oosthuizen, *The Healer-Prophet in Afro-Christian Churches* (Leiden: E. J. Brill, 1992), 43–44, 61–62.

46. B. A. Pauw, *Christianity and Xhosa Tradition: Belief and Ritual among Xhosa-speaking Christians* (New York: Oxford University Press, 1975), 122–23; 126.

47. Interview, Jongile Peter.

48. Interview, Harry Jali, Ndindwa location, 29 April 1974.

49. Interview, Jongile Peter.

50. Statement of Pearce Kaba, 25 April 1923, JD 268 2/950/19.

51. Interview, Harry Jali. On Nongqawuse and the cattle killing, see Peires, *Dead Will Arise.*

Chapter 2

1. Superintendent of Natives, Newlands, Fort Jackson, to Magistrate, East London, 2 June 1922, Cape Archives Depot, Cape Town 1/ELN (East London), vol. 86.

2. Maj. T. Hutchons, Divisional Inspector, South African Police, King William's Town, to Deputy Commissioner, South African Police, Grahamstown, 29 April 1923; statement of F. B. King, 27 May 1923, JD 268 2/950/19.

3. Clement Gladwin to Maj. T. Hutchons, King William's Town, 25 April 1923, JD 268 2/950/19.

4. On the Bulhoek episode, see Robert Edgar, "The Fifth Seal: Enoch Mgijima, the Israelites, and the Bullhoek Massacre," Ph.D. dissertation, University of California, Los Angeles, 1977; Edgar, *Because They Chose the Plan of God: The Story of the Bullhoek Massacre* (Johannesburg: Ravan Press, 1988).

5. Statement of S. J. Jakins, 27 May 1923, JD 289 3/1064/18, part 3.

6. Superintendent of Natives, Berlin, to Magistrate, East London, 19 December 1924, 1/ELN, vol. 86.

7. "Communism in the Union of South Africa," 7 June 1923, JD 289 3/1064/18, part 3.

8. Ibid.

9. Statement of Pearce Kaba; interviews, Jongile Peter and Reuben Tsoko.

10. Tamsanqa eventually succeeded Ngangelizwe in 1939. J. Brand, Magistrate, Middledrift, to Magistrate, King William's Town, 11 April, 1922, State Archives, Pretoria, Bantu Affairs (BAO) 4892 F54/1431/39.

11. Tamsanqa was probably referring to the War of Mlanjeni (1850–53), in which Gqunukwebe levies fought for the British against Ndlambe and Ngqika forces. For their loyal service, the Gqunukwebe were rewarded with land grants around Debe Nek.

12. Statement of Singo Maneli, 15 May 1923; statement of Chief

Uluwonga Kama, 11 May 1923; statement of July Ngaxie, 11 May 1923, JD 268 2/950/19.

13. Statement of Detective Joseph Ngcongolo, Fort White, 13 May 1923, JD 268 2/950/19.

14. Sgt. J. A. Wagenaar, Fort White, to District Commandant, South African Police, King William's Town, 19 August 1923, JD 268 2/950/19.

15. Statement of Joseph Ngcongolo.

16. Statement of Elliott Gara, 8 August 1923, JD 268 2/950/19.

17. There were other religious figures that used locust plagues as evidence of the wrath of God. In late 1922 two Mfengu evangelists, Magqa and Pitwell, circulated throughout the Tsomo, Nqamakwe, and Butterworth areas, electrifying huge crowds with their fire-and-brimstone preaching. Before their anticipated judgment day, they predicted a drought followed by floods and a plague of locusts with iron heads. Then four kings would appear to reveal certain signs. A fierce struggle between Dutch and English would ensue in which the latter would be driven into the sea and exterminated. Finally Africans would do the same to the Dutch and return South Africa to its rightful owners. Although their preaching attracted attention for a limited time, Pitwell remained in the Butterworth area as an evangelist for some time. W. H. C. Taylor, Inspector, South African Police, to Deputy Commissioner, South African Police, Umtata, 2 November 1922; Magistrate, Nqamakwe, to Chief Magistrate, Transkeian Territories, Umtata, 30 October 1922, JD 268 2/950/19.

18. Lt. Colonel H. Kirkpatrick, Deputy Commissioner of Police, Eastern Cape Division, Grahamstown, to South African Police, Pretoria, 13 November 1923, JD 268 2/950/19.

19. J. W. Ord, Acting Magistrate, Middledrift, to Magistrate, King William's Town, 23 October 1923, JD 268 2/950/19.

20. J. N. Daas to Commanding Officer, King William's Town, 2 November 1923, JD 268 2/950/19.

21. W. G. Norman, Sub-Inspector, South African Police, King William's Town to District Commandant, South African Police, East London, 1 November 1923, BAO 6605 11/328.

22. Historians such as William Beinart, Colin Bundy, and Helen Bradford have noted the interpenetration of prophetic and millenarian movements with the ICU in other parts of South Africa in this period. See Beinart and Bundy, *Hidden Struggles*; Helen Bradford,

A Taste of Freedom: The ICU in Rural South Africa, 1924–1930 (New Haven: Yale University Press, 1987).

23. Interview, Jongile Peter.

24. Interview, Tembile Lama, Ngcabasa location, Middledrift, 26 April 1974.

25. Interviews, Jongile Peter and Reuben Tsoko; Robert Edgar, "Garveyism in Africa: Dr. Wellington and the American Movement in the Transkei," *Ufahamu* 6.1 (1976): 31–57; Beinart and Bundy, *Hidden Struggles*, chapter 7.

26. Interview, Tembile Lama.

27. Nontetha's followers did not introduce baptism until around 1940.

28. On Limba's church, see Gary Baines, "'In the World But Not Of It': 'Bishop' Limba and the Church of Christ in New Brighton, c. 1929–1949," *Kronos* 19 (November 1992): 102–34.

Chapter 3

1. Acting Magistrate, King William's Town, to Secretary for Native Affairs, 29 December 1922, BAO 6605 11/328.

2. C. Manganyi, "Making Strange: Race Science and Ethnopsychiatric Discourse," paper presented to the African Studies Institute seminar, University of the Witwatersrand, 15 October 1984, 13.

3. H. J. Deacon, "A History of the Medical Institutions on Robben Island" (Ph.D. dissertation, Cambridge University, 1994), chapter 4; G. H. Burrows, *A History of Medicine in South Africa up to the End of the Nineteenth Century* (Cape Town: A. A. Balkema, 1958), chapter 17.

4. Andrew Scull, *The Most Solitary of Afflictions: Madness and Society in Britain, 1700–1900* (New Haven: Yale University Press, 1993); Scull, "Psychiatry and Social Control in the Nineteenth and Twentieth Centuries," *History of Psychiatry* 2.2 (1991): 149–69.

5. Felicity Swanson, "Colonial Madness: The Construction of Gender in the Grahamstown Lunatic Asylum, 1875–1905" (B.A. [Honours] thesis, University of Cape Town, 1994).

6. It is also noteworthy that official anxiety about incarcerating mentally ill people in prisons was focused on the white population. As the medical superintendent of Pretoria Mental Hospital observed in 1903, "So far as natives are concerned, I do not consider the same

objection applies to their detention in Gaols as in the case of Europeans." Medical Superintendent, Pretoria Mental Asylum, to Secretary to the Law Department, 3 August 1903, State Archives, Pretoria, Law Department (LD) 304 272.

7. Union of South Africa, *Annual Report of the Commissioner for Mental Hygiene,* UG 29-'27.

8. Wulf Sachs, *Black Hamlet: The Mind of an African Negro Revealed by Psychoanalysis* (London: Geoffrey Bles, 1937), 192.

9. Cape of Good Hope, *Reports on Government-Aided Hospitals and Invalid Homes, and Asylums for Lepers and Lunatics and Chronic-Sick Hospitals including Report of the Inspector of Lunatic Asylums for the Calendar Year 1907,* Cape Town, G41-1908.

10. This is the explanation given by Lynette Jackson to a similar phenomenon in colonial Zimbabwe. See her "Gender and Disorder and the Colonial Psychiatric Wards: A Look at the Experience of Mad Black Women in Colonial Southern Rhodesia," paper presented to the history department seminar, University of Zimbabwe, 19 August 1992. One problem with this approach in relation to the eastern Cape is that African women had long dominated the domestic labor market and substantial numbers were thus implicated in a colonial and urban labor market where disruptive or antisocial behaviors would have been detected by white employers and courts. For discussions of gender and the labor system, and the incorporation of Xhosa women into colonial society, see Cherryl Walker, "Gender and the Migrant Labour System"; and J. Cock, "Domestic Service and Education for Domesticity: The Incorporation of Xhosa Women into Colonial Society," in *Women and Gender in Southern Africa to 1945,* ed. Cherryl Walker (London: James Currey, 1990), 76–96, 168–96.

11. Swanson, "Colonial Madness," 42.

12. Magistrate, Middelburg, Cape, to Secretary for Native Affairs, 6 February 1928, Department of Native Affairs (NTS) 10/377.

13. Cited in Alexander Butchart, *The Anatomy of Power: European Constructions of the African Body* (London: Zed Books, 1998), 114. African women who had committed violent acts without any apparent reason were, however, also dispatched to the asylum. Typical crimes were those of infanticide or arson.

14. H. J. Deacon, "Madness, Race, and Moral Treatment: Robben

Island Lunatic Asylum, Cape Colony, 1846–1890," *History of Psychiatry* 7.2 (1996): 287–97; Sally Swartz, "Colonizing the Insane: Causes of Insanity in the Cape, 1891–1920," *History of the Human Sciences* 8.4 (1995): 39–57.

15. In psychiatric circles in late-nineteenth and early-twentieth-century Britain, partly as a result of a growing pessimism about the capacity of asylums to deliver "cures," new theoretical accounts for madness and all forms of deviation from conventional morality emerged. Some psychiatrists argued that dissolution and depravity exacted a heavy biological price on the European race, resulting in the progressive "degradation of nervous tissue" and that constitutional defects were transmitted to succeeding generations, bringing crime, madness, idiocy, sterility, and death in their train. Asylums were justified as vital institutions in maintaining social order through sequestering the disruptive, while psychiatrists also shifted their domain into the field of prevention, such as in the schools, factories, families, and armies. The increasing emphasis on heredity in psychiatry, moreover, brought it into a close relationship with eugenic ideas. Scull, "Psychiatry and Social Control." For a discussion of the South African colonial inflections of these tendencies, see Sally Swartz, "Colonizing the Insane," 39; Swanson, "Colonial Madness"; Linda Chisholm, "Gender and Deviance in South African Industrial Schools and Reformatories for Girls, 1911–1934" in *Women and Gender in Southern Africa to 1945*, ed. Cherryl Walker (London: James Currey, 1990), 293–312; and Saul Dubow, *Scientific Racism in Modern South Africa* (Cambridge: Cambridge University Press, 1995), 16, 144, 154, 163, 166–67.

16. Dubow, *Scientific Racism*, 197–209.

17. T. D. Greenlees, "Insanity among the Natives in the Cape Colony," *Journal of Mental Science* 41 (1895), 71.

18. Acting Medical Superintendent, Weskoppies Asylum, to Assistant Colonial Secretary, 17 February 1910, State Archives, Pretoria, Colonial Secretary (CS) 930/19017.

19. Dubow, *Scientific Racism*, 169–70. Well into the twentieth century, many psychiatric practitioners implied that urbanization itself was "psychopathogenic" and that the "urbanized black" was somehow in a state of transition and alienated from the "natural" (rural) state of black people. See Leslie Swartz, "Issues for Cross Cultural

Psychiatric Research in South Africa," *Culture, Medicine, and Psychiatry* 9.1 (1985): 59–74.

20. Secretary for Native Affairs to Assistant Colonial Secretary, 11 February 1910, CS 930/19017.

21. Medical Superintendent, Pretoria Asylum, to Secretary, Law Department, Transvaal, 29 November 1903, LD 67 272/03.

22. J. Conry, "Insanity among Natives in the Cape Colony," *South African Medical Record* 5 (1907), 36.

23. Laubscher, *Sex, Custom and Psychopathology*, chapters 3 and 10.

24. Alfred T. Bryant, *Zulu Medicine and Medicine-Men* (Cape Town: C. Struik, 1966), 70.

25. Sachs, *Black Hamlet*, 187–88; Laubscher, *Sex, Custom, and Psychopathology*, 227.

26. W. J. Davis, *A Dictionary of the Kaffir Language Including the Xosa and Zulu Dialects* (London: Wesleyan Mission House, 1923); A. Fisher, E. Weiss, E. Mdala, and S. Tshabe, *English-Xhosa Dictionary* (Cape Town: Oxford University Press, 1985). See also G. Drennan, A. Levett, and L. Swartz, "Hidden Dimensions of Power and Resistance in the Translation Process: A South African Study," *Culture, Medicine, and Psychiatry* 15.3 (1991): 361–81.

27. Bryant, *Zulu Medicine*, 70–71.

28. Ibid., 70–73; Oosthuizen, *Healer-Prophet*. Another term for African cultural diseases used by cross-cultural psychiatrists is "culture bound syndromes," a designation that does not conform to the most widely used Western diagnostic system—*The Diagnostic and Statistical Manual of Mental Disorders* (4th ed., American Psychiatric Association, 1994 [DSM-IV])—which described them as "localized, folk, diagnostic categories that frame coherent meanings for certain repetitive, patterned, and troubling sets of experiences and observations." See Leslie Swartz, *Culture and Mental Health: A Southern African View* (Cape Town: Oxford University Press, 1998), 154.

29. Sachs, *Black Hamlet*, 183–88.

30. Henri Phillipe Junod, *Revenge or Reformation? A Study of the South African Prison System with Special Reference to Africans*, Christian Council Study Series (Lovedale: Lovedale Press, 1944), 5.

31. Sachs, *Black Hamlet*, 187, 191–93.

32. Union of South Africa, *Report of the Mental Hospitals Departmental Committee*, 1936–1937 (UG 36–'37), 10.

33. Ray E. Phillips, *The Bantu in the City: A Study of Cultural Adjustment on the Witwatersrand* (Lovedale: Lovedale Press, 1938), chapter 3. The phrase "quest for therapy" is used to convey the pluralistic and syncretistic characters of African healing cultures and is taken from John M. Janzen, with William Arkinstall, *The Quest for Therapy in Lower Zaire: Medical Pluralism in Lower Zaire* (Berkeley: University of California Press, 1978). South African anthropologists have demonstrated that in South Africa, as in Zaire, systems of therapy have arisen that incorporate both the "traditional" and the "modern," and that this was made possible by "the extraordinary openness of traditional practitioners and public to new theories and a refusal to be limited by a monistic picture of illness." As Janzen puts it: "Western medicine's unique competence was accepted and appreciated, but not at the expense of tradition-derived therapies." See Hammond-Tooke, *Rituals and Medicines*, 153.

34. Charlie Fukela Nkele to Secretary for Native Affairs, 11 February 1958, NTS 9303 5/376.

35. Harriet Ngubane, "Clinical Practice and Organization of Indigenous Healers in South Africa," *Social Science and Medicine* 15B (1981): 361–66.

36. Laura Longmore, *The Dispossessed: A Study of the Sex-Life of Bantu Women in Urban Areas in and around Johannesburg* (London: Corgi Books, 1959), 232.

37. Harriet Ngubane, *Body and Mind in Zulu Medicine* (New York: Academic Press, 1977); Harriet Sibisi (Ngubane), "The Place of Spirit Possession in Zulu Cosmology," in *Religion and Social Change in Southern Africa: Anthropological Essays in Honour of Monica Wilson*, ed. Michael Whisson and Martin West (Cape Town: David Philip, 1975); Bryant, *Zulu Medicine*, 71–72; Patrick Harries, *Work, Culture, and Identity: Migrant Laborers in Mozambique and South Africa, c. 1860–1910* (Portsmouth, N.H.: Heinemann, 1994), 163–66; Marks, *'Not Either an Experimental Doll,'* 54–55.

38. Hammond-Tooke, *Rituals and Medicines*, 128.

39. Harries, *Work, Culture, and Identity*, 163–65.

40. Ngubane, *Body and Mind*, 147.

41. I. M. Lewis, *Ecstatic Religion: An Anthropological Study of Spirit Possession and Shamanism* (Harmondsworth: Penguin Books, 1971), cited in Hammond-Tooke, *Rituals and Medicines*, 135.

42. A. F. Matibela to Secretary for Public Health, 15 June 1932,

State Archives Depot, Department of Health (GES) 1763 25/30D. We are grateful to Catherine Burns for this reference.

43. Union of South Africa, *Report of the Mental Hospitals Departmental Committee 1936–1937* (UG 36-'37), 21.

44. Anne Mager, "Gender and the Making of the Ciskei, 1945–1959" (Ph.D. dissertation, University of Cape Town, 1995), 5–6.

45. The 1918 act, which replaced the previous lunacy legislation governing the former colonies and republics, was set up to cover a person who, "in consequence of mental disorder or disease or permanent defect of reason or mind, . . . is incapable of managing himself or his affairs . . . or is in danger to himself and others . . . or requires supervision, treatment and control . . . or . . . a child [who] appears to be permanently incapable of receiving proper benefit from the instruction of ordinary schools." The categories set up included mental disorder, "mental inferiority," epilepsy, and "moral imbecility." The law courts had the authority to determine mental disorder or defectiveness. No person could be detained except by order of a magistrate, court, or judge. The magistrate was required to gain the assistance of two medical practitioners, and the medical certificates had to be issued within fourteen days. The reception order was valid for up to six weeks. See A. Kruger, *Mental Health Law in South Africa* (Durban: Butterworths, 1980).

46. Deacon, "Medical Institutions on Robben Island," chapter 4.

47. Swanson, "Colonial Madness," 49.

48. Sally Swartz, "The Black Insane in the Cape, 1891–1920," *Journal of Southern African Studies* 21.3 (1995): 410.

49. Cape of Good Hope, *Report of the Select Committee on the Treatment of Lunatics* (SC [Select Committee] 14–13), appendices.

50. Cape of Good Hope, *Report on Government-Aided Hospitals and Invalid Homes*, G41–1908. We thank Felicity Swanson for sharing her insights and knowledge of the early Fort Beaufort Asylum. Personal Communication to Hilary Sapire, March 1999.

51. Union of South Africa, *Annual Report of the Commissioner for Mentally Disordered and Defective Persons*, 1922–1923, U.G. 36-'24.

52. *Martello*, no. 77 (October 1994): 3. *Martello* is the magazine produced by the Fort Beaufort Museum.

53. Office of the Mental Hospital, Pretoria, to Commissioner for Mental Hygiene, Pretoria, 2 June 1930, BAO 6605 11/328.

54. The category dementia praecox had emerged as a consequence

of the Kraepelinian revolution of the late nineteenth century, in which dementia praecox was distinguished from manic depressive psychosis. In turn, it would be replaced by the term schizophrenia. By 1918, dementia praecox was in general use in Cape hospitals and by the 1920s was the most common form of mental illness diagnosed across all mental hospitals in South Africa. It was divided into hebephrenia, catatonia, paranoia, and simplex. It was never universally accepted, however; many psychiatrists preferred the term schizophrenia, which had been introduced by the Swiss psychiatrist Eugen Bleuler in 1911. The latter term allowed for improvement or arrest and implied that these disorders need not all inevitably progress to terminal dementia, in line with Kraepelin's views. E. Hare, "The Two Manias: A Study of the Evolution of the Modern Concept of Mania," *British Journal of Psychiatry* 88 (1981): 89–96. For a detailed discussion of changing classifications in South African mental hospitals, see Sally Swartz, "Changing Diagnoses in Valkenberg Asylum, Cape Colony, 1891–1920," *History of Psychiatry* 6.4 (1995): 431–51.

55. D. K. Henderson and R. D. Gillespie, *A Textbook of Psychiatry for Students and Practitioners* (Oxford: Oxford University Press, 1927), 201–2.

56. Certainly, by the 1930s, some South African writers believed that the patterns of African psychotic behavior were broadly similar to those presented by Europeans. B. J. F. Laubscher claimed that African schizophrenics all conformed to the classical paranoid, catatonic, and hebephrenic types. He said that the only difference in patterns of behavior between Africans and Europeans was the "delusional content" and the predominance of active, "negativist types." See Laubscher, *Sex, Custom, and Psychopathology*, 275. The psychoanalytically trained psychiatrist Wulf Sachs went further in arguing for equivalence, observing that the "delusions, and hallucinations of the insane native were in structure, in origin and, partly in content, similar to those of the European." Wulf Sachs, "The Insane Native: An Introduction to a Psychological Study," *South African Journal of Science* 30 (1933): 710.

57. *Martello* 77 (October 1994): 9–10. This section also draws on information provided by Felicity Swanson (personal communication to Hilary Sapire, March 1999).

58. Erving Goffman, *Asylums: Essays on the Social Situation of Mental Patients and Other Inmates* (Garden City, N.Y.: Anchor Books,

1961). T. D. Moodie describes a "moral economy" that emerged in the mining compounds of the Witwatersrand, by which certain obligations were expected from mine officials and authority figures, such as certain minimal standards in food, wages comparable to those at other mines, a limit on personal assault underground, fair adjudication of personal disputes, and latitude in allowing workers privacy in the domain of recreation and sexuality. T. Dunbar Moodie, with Vivienne Ndatshe, *Going for Gold: Men, Mines, and Migration* (Los Angeles: University of California Press, 1994), chapter 3.

59. Physician Superintendent, Fort Beaufort Mental Hospital, to Commissioner for Mental Hygiene, 21 January 1943, BAO 6681 170/332.

60. Admission register, Weskoppies Mental Hospital, Pretoria.

61. Interview, Henry Jali.

62. Medical Superintendent, Pretoria Asylum, to Secretary to the Transvaal Administration, 11 April 1901, CS 10 1044.

63. Waltraud Ernst, *Mad Tales from the Raj: The European Insane in British India, 1800–1858* (London: Routledge, 1991).

64. A. J. Olivier, "Weskoppies Hospitaal, 1891–1966," unpublished paper, n.d.

65. Charlotte Searle, *The History of the Development of Nursing in South Africa, 1652–1960: A Socio-Historical Survey* (Pretoria: South African Nursing Association, 1965), chapter 8; C. Plug and J. L. Roos, "Weskoppies Hospital, Founded 1892: The Early Years," *South African Medical Journal* 81 (1992): 218–21; "Facilities Available for Treatment in Mental Hospitals and Institutions for the Feebleminded with Brief Reference to Extra-Mural Work Done by Government Psychiatrists," memo by Commissioner for Mental Hygiene, August 1952, University of the Witwatersrand, Freed papers, A1212/D3.

66. J. T. Dunston is a key figure both in this story, and in South Africa's history of psychiatry. Born, educated, and trained in England, he became a medical officer at the Pretoria asylum and medical superintendent of that institution in 1908. He was a moving force in the drafting of the Mental Disorders Act of 1916. He was appointed Commissioner of Mental Disorder and Defectives in accordance with the terms of this legislation and, in 1922, became Commissioner for Mental Hygiene. He was the chief professional advisory officer to the Minister of the Interior and the first professor of psychiatry at the University of the Witwatersrand. With Dunston at the helm, the number of mental health institutions and psychiatric services in-

creased markedly. Influenced by contemporary thinking in Europe, Britain, and the United States, he was also a prime mover in the establishment of the South African National Council for Mental Hygiene. See M. Minde, "History of Mental Health Services in South Africa," part 7, "Services since Union," *South African Medical Journal* 49.11 (1975): 405–9; Dubow, *Scientific Racism*, 147–49, 151, 173, 233.

67. Physician Superintendent, Weskoppies, to Commissioner for Mental Hygiene, 18 January 1938, State Archives, Pretoria, Superintendent, Weskoppies Hospital (SWH). The predominance of African men in the hospital must have a great deal to do with the drastically skewed demographic profile of the Rand, one of the hospital's catchment areas, where until the 1940s, African men significantly outnumbered women. The authors of the 1937 report on mental hospitals suggested that economic pressures made it more likely for male rather than female members of households to end up in mental hospitals, but they do not offer concrete evidence for this assertion.

68. Director of Native Labour to Secretary of Native Affairs, Central Archives Depot, Government Native Labour Bureau (GNLB) 85 3635.

69. Pass Officer, Johannesburg, to Director of Native Labour, Johannesburg, 12 August 1927, GNLB 85 3635 / 12 / 829.

70. Governor-General Decision Patients on Register, Pretoria Mental Hospital, circa 1936, SWH 1 1/3.

71. Edgar, *African American in South Africa*, 188–89. The impressions of the asylum attendant cited in Ralph Bunche's diary powerfully echoes the views of municipal administrators of this period, who were struggling to contain a massive influx of Africans into the urban areas and to counter the perceived threat this posed to existing mechanisms of social control. They also parallel the anxieties expressed by psychiatrists in east and central Africa about the threat of "disintegration" of traditional structures of African societies and the dangers of industrialization, education, and urbanization. See Megan Vaughan's discussion of colonial psychiatry and of the assertion that "deculturation" lay behind the increase in African mental illness from the 1930s to the 1950s. Megan Vaughan, *Curing Their Ills: Colonial Power and African Illness* (London: Polity Press, 1991), chapter 5.

72. Secretary for Native Affairs to Secretary for Interior, 7 October 1943, NTS 9306/377.

73. F. D. Crosthwaite, Physician Superintendent, Pretoria Mental

Hospital, to Commissioner for Mental Hygiene, 2 June 1930, BAO 6605 11/328.

74. Sachs, *Black Hamlet*, 191; see also Jonathan Sadowsky, "Insanity and the Problem of Hegemony: 'Cases' from Colonial Nigeria," paper presented to the Department of Anthropology, University of the Witwatersrand, 1995, 8–11.

75. Brian Willan, "An African in Kimberley: Sol T. Plaatje, 1894–1898," in *Industrialisation and Social Change in South Africa*, ed. Shula Marks and Richard Rathbone (London: Longman, 1982), 242–43. See also Leon de Kock, *Civilising Barbarians: Missionary Narrative and African Textual Response in Nineteenth-Century South Africa* (Johannesburg: Witwatersrand University Press, 1996). Similarly, Queen Victoria recurred in Kenyan political discourse as a symbol of an early colonial alliance of progress between Africans and British that had later been abrogated by rapacious white settlers and an oppressive colonial administration. John Lonsdale argues that she inhabited an imagined past of mutual obligation by which Kenyans attempted to shame colonial administrators into a political dialogue. See John Lonsdale, "The Prayers of Waikyaki: Political Uses of the Kikuyu Past," in *Revealing Prophets: Prophecy in Eastern African History*, ed. David Anderson and Douglas Johnson (Athens: Ohio University Press, 1995), 245–46, 273–74. We are grateful to both John Lonsdale and Leon de Kock for their suggestions and references, courtesy of the discussion network H-AFRICA.

76. F. A. Mouton, *Voices in the Desert: Margaret and William Ballinger, A Biography* (Pretoria: Benedic Books, 1997), 146.

77. Secretary for the Interior to Secretary for Native Affairs, 16 May 1928, BAO 6605 11/328.

Chapter 4

1. An early use of the pilgrimage of grace was during a sixteenth-century uprising in Northern England, when rebels petitioned the crown for a redress of their grievances. See Michael Bush, *The Pilgrimage of Grace: A Study of the Rebel Armies of October 1536* (Manchester: Manchester University Press, 1996). The phrase *pilgrimage of grace* was applied to the march of Nontetha's followers by South African journalists.

2. This account is derived from interviews with Reuben Tsoko

and Jongile Peter, a written statement of Reuben Tsoko, and a document, "Uhambo lwase Pitoli" [Journey to Pretoria], compiled by members of the Church of the Prophetess Nontetha around 1990.

3. Interview, Tobi Nokrawuzana, July 1997.

4. Interview, Jongile Peter. Gola was the name of the headman in Nontetha's area.

5. Interview, Tobi Nokrawuzana.

6. Ibid.

7. *Daily Dispatch* (East London), 14 January and 2 February 1927; *Rand Daily Mail* (Johannesburg), 10 February 1927.

8. Chief Native Commissioner, King William's Town, to Secretary for Native Affairs, Pretoria, 16 April 1928, BAO 6605 11/328.

9. "Followers of the Prophetess," *Daily Dispatch*, 5 March 1930.

10. Inspector, Office of the District Commandant, SAP, Aliwal North, to Deputy Commissioner, SAP, Grahamstown, 28 March 1930, BAO 6605 11/328.

11. Ibid.

12. Office of the Chief Native Inspector, King William's Town, to Secretary for Native Affairs, 10 April 1930, BAO 6605 11/328.

13. "The Crazy Prophetess: Earthly Confidante of Queen Victoria," *Daily Dispatch*, 26 February 1930.

14. D. W. Ntsikana to J. B. M. Hertzog, 10 December 1927, BAO 6605 11/328.

15. Delanto Qoshe to Native Affairs Department, 10 January 1933, BAO 6605 11/328.

16. Charles Crabtree, Secretary, Aliwal North Welfare Society, to Minister of Native Affairs, 14 March 1930, BAO 6605 11/328.

17. "Nontete," *Umteteli wa Bantu* (Johannesburg), 19 July 1930.

18. This points to the notorious inexactitude of psychiatrists' diagnoses of African mental patients. However, it should be noted that even in contemporary Britain and the United States, diagnoses of schizophrenia have often not been clear and there are strong arguments that current treatments are hardly efficacious, and are often damaging.

19. F. D. Crosthwaite, Physician Superintendent, Pretoria Mental Hospital to Commissioner of Mental Hygiene, 2 June 1930, BAO 6605 11/328. For a discussion on religion and psychiatry, see M. Lipsedge, "Religion and Madness in History," in *Psychiatry and Religion: Context, Consensus, and Controversies*, ed. Dinesh Bhugra (London:

Routledge, 1995), 23–47. Whereas the early Christian tradition saw "religious madness" as the enviable ecstasy of the visionary or mystic, by the twentieth century this would be regarded with suspicion by doctors and police. "Good" religious madness was changed by the authorities, polite society, doctors, and scientists into the "psychopathology" of "bad" religious melancholy. See Roy Porter, "The Prophetic Body: Lady Eleonor Davies and the Meanings of Madness," *Women's Writing* 1 (1994): 51–54.

20. Henderson and Gillespie, *Textbook of Psychiatry*, 212.

21. In this instance, despite some of their limitations, the insights from some of the antipsychiatry literature is apposite, notably from those writers who argue that the category *mental illness* and other psychiatric diagnoses are often convenient labels attached to individuals who have violated conventional behavioral norms, but who cannot be slotted into recognized categories of deviance. Once thus labeled by representatives of dominant social groups, the individual is committed to a mental hospital and, in turn, the very process of institutionalization transforms his or her self-conceptions, creating a form of secondary deviance. In other words, labeling or stigmatizing individuals as mentally ill produces disturbed behavior. The individual is socialized to conform to the "crazy" role, and thereby to reinforce the label. Diagnoses of mental illness, according to these theories, reveal less about the patient and more about the social system, the reaction of others to unconventional behaviors, and the official agencies of control and treatment. For the classic statement of labeling theory, see Thomas J. Scheff, *Being Mentally Ill: A Sociological Theory* (Chicago: Aldine, 1966). Labeling theories often contend that "mental illness" is the peculiar creation of modern, industrialized Western societies. For a thoughtful discussion of the applicability of labeling theory in colonial contexts, see Jonathan Sadowsky, *Imperial Bedlam: Institutions of Madness in Colonial Southwest Nigeria* (Berkeley: University of California Press, 1999), chapter 1.

22. According to Henderson and Gillespie, patients who are aware that they held delusional beliefs and could acknowledge this were more amenable to treatment than those who did not. See Henderson and Gillespie, *Textbook of Psychiatry*, 89.

23. The official policy was to release patients either when they had been restored to a state of mental health and "reasonable normality" and able to participate in social life or return to their fami-

lies without constituting a danger to themselves or to their societies. See Union of South Africa, *Mental Hospitals Departmental Committee.*

24. By 1938 there were 1,663 patients in Weskoppies Hospital. Of these, 761 were black (537 men and 224 women). See Physician Superintendent to Commissioner for Mental Hygiene, Pretoria, 18 January 1938, State Archives, Pretoria, Records of Weskoppies Hospital, (SWH) 2, Annual Reports.

25. "Nontete," *Umteteli wa Bantu*, 19 July 1930.

26. Consider, for example, the demise of categories such as "hysteria," neurasthenia, and "acute mania." See Mark Micale, "Hysteria and Its Historiography," *History of Science* 27.3 (1989): 223–61; D. Kennedy, "The Perils of the Midday Sun: Climatic Anxieties in the Colonial Tropics," in *The Empire of Nature: Hunting, Conservation, and British Imperialism,* ed. John MacKenzie (Manchester: Manchester University Press, 1988), 118–40.

27. Sally Swartz, "Colonizing the Insane," 40.

28. Edgar, *African American in South Africa*, 188; Sachs, *Black Hamlet*, 189.

29. Edgar, *African American in South Africa*, 189.

30. The purpose of the farm on the hospital estate was to enable the institute to be self-sufficient and to contribute to the tranquil, pastoral atmosphere that early asylum reformers deemed to be so essential to patient well-being. See Union of South Africa, *Mental Hospitals Departmental Committee*, 8.

31. "Facilities Available for the Treatment in Mental Hospitals and Institutions for the Feebleminded with Brief Reference to Extra-Mural Work done by Government Psychiatrists," Memo by Commissioner for Mental Hygiene, L. F. Freed Papers, A1212/D3, University of the Witwatersrand. As the commissioner for mental hygiene observed, "many of the patients suffered from toxic psychosis in addition to the psychosis which was the cause of their being admitted to the hospital."

32. Union of South Africa, *Mental Hospitals Departmental Committee*, 7.

33. Union of South Africa, *Report by Mr. Pienaar on Charges of Ill-Treatment Made by Ernest Francois Maas and Others against Certain Warders of the Mental Hospital at Pretoria, 1923*, A2–'23.

34. J. E. Baird to Governor General, 13 May 1929, State Archives, Governor General (GG) 1249 33/1828.

35. Physician Superintendent, Pretoria Mental Hospital, to Secretary for the Interior, 8 August 1936, SWH A3/55.

36. Secretary for the Interior to Secretary for Native Affairs, 24 March 1931, NTS 11/377.

Chapter 5

1. See Shula Marks's comments in this regard in her "The Context of Personal Narrative: Reflections on *'Not Either an Experimental Doll': The Separate Worlds of Three South African Women,"* in *Interpreting Women's Lives: Feminist Theory and Personal Narratives,* ed. Personal Narrative Group (Bloomington: Indiana University Press, 1989): 39–55.

2. Newclare Cemetery Register, May 1935, Rebecca Street Cemetery Office, Pretoria.

3. BAO 6605 11/328. The procedure of burying African mental hospital inmates without coffins was a controversial one. In 1923, for example, the Queenstown Advisory Board protested against this practice, urging the Queenstown town council to ensure that all Africans were afforded "a decent burial." Whereas "civilized natives" who died in mental hospitals in the eastern Cape were buried in coffins, at Weskoppies Hospital, unless special requests were made by the deceased's family, the policy was to bury all Africans, regardless of their economic and social status, in blankets rather than coffins. See Acting Secretary of the Interior to Secretary for Native Affairs, 27 August 1923, NTS 3/377.

4. Interview, Reuben Tsoko, April 1974. The government was opposed to paying about £12 for a coffin made of sheet-metal, £5 for the cemetery fee, and £15 for transporting the body to Middledrift. The government also balked at releasing her body because they had to observe official authorization and a Department of Health rule that stipulated that "except in special circumstances . . . no recommendation for the issue of a permit for exhumation will be made . . . by the Union Health Department until at least two years after interment." BAO 6605 11/328.

5. Robert Edgar, discussion with church members of the Church of the Prophetess Nontetha, Thamarha location, 11 August 1998.

6. Unsigned memorandum of 1955, BAO 6605 11/328.

7. Edgar, discussion with church and family members, Thamarha, 11 August 1998.

8. Newclare Cemetery Register, May 1935.

9. The deputy director of the office is Ndumiso Gola, who grew up in Nontetha's village, Khulile, with some of Nontetha's grandchildren. He had heard their stories about their grandmother and her fate in the mental asylum. Therefore, he welcomed our investigation of her grave site.

10. Directorate of Museums and Heritage Resources, *Announcement of Directorate of Museums and Heritage Resources of Community Heritage Projects.*

11. After the exhumation, officials were able to identify additional money to assist with the costs of the reburial ceremony.

12. We have based this section on newspaper accounts from the *Daily Dispatch* (East London), 24 August 1996, 24 November 1996, and 26 February 1996; *Weekly Mail and Guardian*, 5 March and 29 March 1996.

13. *Daily Dispatch*, 6 January 1996.

14. We thank Michael Blakey of Howard University and Trefor Jenkins and Phillip Tobias of the University of the Witwatersrand for educating us about procedures and options.

15. "Unearthing Our Hidden History: 'Nkosi Sikelel'i Africa,'" *Teacher Resource Page*, September 1996; A. E. Buff, "In Search of Enoch Sontonga: Author and Composer of 'Nkosi Sikelel'i Africa,'" Report for the Greater Johannesburg Transitional Metropolitan Council, April 1996. We thank Luli Callinicos for sharing these documents with us.

16. M. Steyn and C. Nienaber, *Report on the Excavation and Analysis of Skeleton UP 90 (Presumed to Be That of Nonteta Bungu)* (August 1998), 3–4.

17. *Sowetan*, 29 June 1998; *Cape Times*, 26 June 1998; *Eastern Province Herald*, 23 June 1998; and *Pretoria News*, 23 June 1998. For problems with the MK exhumations and other burials, see Charles van Onselen, "Dead But Not Quite Buried," *London Review of Books* 20.21 (29 October 1998): 23–24.

18. Nokrawuzana observed that she felt more tired after this journey than when she walked for two months in 1927.

19. Maureen Isaacson, "The Search for a Lost Prophet," *Sunday Independent*, 19 July 1998.

20. Ibid.

21. Steyn and Nienaber, *Report on the Excavation and Analysis.*

22. Edgar, discussion with church and family members, 11 August 1998.

23. Mamphela Ramphele points out how, in the larger drama of community funerals of the 1980s, the needs of the group often took precedence over those of individual mourners who had lost a family member in the political violence of that period. See Ramphele, "Political Widowhood in South Africa: The Embodiment of Ambiguity," *Daedalus* 125.1 (1996): 108. See also Leslie Swartz, *Culture and Mental Health*, 182–83; Garrey Dennie, "The Cultural Politics of Burial in South Africa, 1884–1990" (Ph.D. dissertation, Johns Hopkins University, 1997).

24. "Bring Back the Hottentot Venus," *Weekly Mail and Guardian*, 15 June 1995; "Hope of Saartje's Return Won't Die," *Weekly Mail and Guardian*, 15 December 1995; "Returning Humanity to Dry Bones," *Weekly Mail and Guardian*, 22 February 1996. Sara Bartman was a Khoisan woman born in the eastern Cape in the early 1790s. In 1810 she was brought to England and exhibited to the public. Outraged evangelical abolitionists, however, took Bartman's keepers to court, objecting to the lewd nature of the exhibition and to her unfree status. The case was lost and Bartman was subsequently removed to the provinces and thence to Paris in 1814. There she aroused scientific interest and was examined by a team of French scientists in the following years. Upon her death, shortly thereafter, her body was dissected by a team of scientists and her remains preserved. Until recently, her genitalia were exhibited at the Musèe de l'Homme in Paris. If Bartman was reduced by scientists and museum visitors to a collection of sexual parts, Yvette Abrahams has argued that through their fixation on Bartman as a symbol, sexual metaphor, and scientific specimen, contemporary scholars have lost sight altogether of Bartman the woman and of her immediate social context. This, she says, has obscured from view the likelihood that Bartman was a slave. See Yvette Abrahams, "Disempowered to Consent: Sara Bartman and Khoisan Slavery in the Nineteenth Century Cape Colony and Britain," *South African Historical Journal* 35 (November 1996): 89–114. Other scholarly articles on Bartman as "circus freak" and scientific specimen include Sander Gilman, "Black Bodies, White Bodies: Towards an Iconography of Female Sexuality in Late Nineteenth Century

Art, Medicine, and Literature," in *"Race," Writing, and Difference*, ed. Henry Louis Gates (Chicago: University of Chicago Press, 1986), 223–61 and Stephen Jay Gould, *The Flamingo's Smile: Reflections in Natural History* (New York: Norton, 1985).

25. "Bushman's Head Found in British Museums," *Weekly Mail and Guardian*, 2 February 1996.

26. Shula Marks, "Rewriting South African History; or, the Hunt for Hintsa's Head," Seventh Annual Bindoff Lecture, Queen Mary and Westfield College, University of London, 12 March 1996.

27. *Sunday Independent*, 19 July 1998.

28. See Donald McNeil Jr.'s account of the funeral, "South Africa Restores a Prophetess to Her People," *New York Times*, 18 November 1998.

29. For discussions on public history commemorations that become events in themselves, see Albert Grundlingh and Hilary Sapire, "From Feverish Festival to Repetitive Ritual? The Changing Fortunes of 'Great Trek' Mythology in an Industrialising South Africa," *South African Historical Journal* 21 (1989): 19–38; Ciraj Rassool and Leslie Witz, "The 1952 Jan van Riebeeck Tercentenary Festival: Constructing and Contesting Public National History in South Africa," *Journal of African History* 34 (1993): 447–68.

Conclusion

1. John Comaroff and Jean Comaroff, "The Madman and the Migrant," in *Ethnography and the Historical Imagination*, ed. John Comaroff and Jean Comaroff (Boulder, Colo.: Westview Press, 1992), 103; Sadowsky, "Insanity and the Problem of Hegemony."

2. Bengt Sundkler, "African Church History in a New Key," in *Religion, Development, and African Identity*, ed. Kirsten Petersen (Uppsala: Scandinavian Institute of African Studies, 1987), 73.

3. Hildegarde Fast, "'In at One Ear and Out at the Other': African Responses to the Wesleyan Message in Xhosaland, 1825–1835," *Journal of Religion in Africa* 23.2 (1993): 147–74. See also Fast's M.A. thesis, "African Perceptions of the Missionaries and Their Message: Wesleyans at Mount Coke and Butterworth, 1825–35" (University of Cape Town, 1991). For a discussion on the state of the historiography, see Norman Etherington, "Recent Trends in the Historiogra-

phy of Christianity in Southern Africa," *Journal of Southern African Studies* 22.2 (1996): 201–20.

4. See Robert Hefner's introduction to his edited volume, *Conversion to Christianity: Historical and Anthropological Perspectives on a Great Transformation* (Berkeley: University of California Press, 1993). See also Terence Ranger's essay, "The Local and the Global in Southern African Religious History," in the same volume.

5. Andrew Walls, *The Missionary Movement in Christian History: Studies in the Transmission of Faith* (Maryknoll, N.Y.: Orbis Books, 1982), 27–29.

6. Sundkler, "African Church History," 80.

7. Hammond-Tooke, *Rituals and Medicines*, 118; Sundkler, *Bantu Prophets in South Africa*, 22.

8. See Harold Scheub, "And So I Grew Up: The Autobiography of Nongenile Masithathu Zenani," in *Life Histories of African Women*, ed. Patricia W. Romero (Atlantic Highlands, N.J.: Ashfield Press, 1988), 7–45.

9. As many anthropologists have pointed out, women's status in such kin-based systems was situational, influenced by factors such as lineage position and age, rather than by inherent gender categories. See Iris Berger's important discussion of the anthropological and historical literature on women and gender in southern Africa: "'Beasts of Burden' Revisited: Interpretations of Women and Gender in Southern African Societies," in *Paths Toward the Past: African Historical Essays in Honor of Jan Vansina*, ed. R. W. Harms, J. C. Miller, D. S. Newbury, and M. D. Wagner (Atlanta: African Studies Association Press, 1994), 126–41. We are grateful to Iris Berger for her comments on the significance of Nontetha's age. Iris Berger, personal communication, 8 June 1998.

10. Belinda Bozzoli, with Mmantho Nkotsoe, *Women of Phokeng: Consciousness, Life Strategy, and Migrancy in South Africa, 1900–1983* (Johannesburg: Ravan Press, 1991); Mager, "Gender and the Making of the Ciskei"; Helen Bradford, "Women, Gender, and Colonialism: Rethinking the History of the British Cape Colony and Its Frontier Zones, c. 1806–1870," *Journal of African History* 27 (1996): 351–70; Cherryl Walker, ed., *Women and Gender in Southern Africa to 1945* (London, James Currey, 1990); and Berger, "'Beasts of Burden' Revisited."

11. Berger, "'Beasts of Burden' Revisited," 138–39.

12. See William Beinart and Colin Bundy, "The Union, the Nation, and the Talking Crow: The Ideology and Tactics of the Independent ICU in East London," in *Hidden Struggles in Rural South Africa*, ed. William Beinart and Colin Bundy (Johannesburg: Ravan Press, 1987), 270–320.

13. A particularly dramatic illustration of the ways in which gender relations could be challenged in small towns in Natal in this period by female activism is provided in Helen Bradford's "'We Are Now the Men': Women's Beer Protests in the Natal Countryside, 1929," in *Class, Community, and Conflict: South African Perspectives*, ed. Belinda Bozzoli (Johannesburg: Ravan Press, 1987), 292–323. In the beer protests, in addition to demonstrating their antagonism to the discriminatory practices of white officialdom (in dressing as men), women appropriated the cultural forms that generally expressed male dominance.

However, it is not as though urban African women fully resolved these contradictions in their lives and roles either. In a fascinating paper about Nontsizi Mgqwetho, an urban Xhosa female poet writing in the 1920s, Jeff Opland discusses the ways in which her poetry encompasses these contradictions. On the one hand, these poems express female frustration at male hegemony, yet, in decrying aspects of white exploitation and urging a return to "traditional" values, her protest as an outraged woman is swamped by the voice of an anti-white traditionalist that sought to confirm, rather than challenge, the gender hierarchy. Jeff Opland, "Nontsizi Mgqwetho: Xhosa Woman Newspaper Poet of the 1920s," paper presented to the Gender in Empire and Commonwealth Seminar, Institute of Commonwealth Studies, London, 3 November 1994.

14. Beinart and Bundy, *Hidden Struggles*, 270–320.

15. Crais, "Representation and the Politics of Identity."

16. Beinart and Bundy, *Hidden Struggles*, 294.

17. Quoted ibid., 314.

18. Inspector, CID, Marshall Square, Johannesburg to Deputy Commissioner, SAP, Witwatersrand Division, 21 August 1923; 15 August 1923, SAP 6/953/23/3.

19. Stephen Clingman, "Beyond the Limit: The Social Relations of Madness in Southern African Fiction," unpublished paper, African Studies Institute, University of the Witwatersrand, 3 October 1988; Bessie Head, *A Question of Power* (London: Heinemann, 1974); Liz

Gunner, "Mothers, Daughters, and Madness in the Work by Four Women Writers: Bessie Head, Jean Rhys, Ama Ata Aidoo, and Tsitsi Dangarembga," unpublished paper, n.d.; Franz Fanon, *Black Skin, White Masks* (New York: Grove Press, 1967); Vaughan, *Curing Their Ills;* Megan Vaughan, "Madness and Colonialism, Colonialism as Madness: Re-Reading Fanon," paper presented to the Association of African Studies of the United Kingdom, Stirling University, 1991; Sadowsky, "Imperial Bedlam."

20. Interest is rapidly growing in the history of psychiatry in South Africa. See Marks, *'Not Either an Experimental Doll';* Swanson, "Colonial Madness"; Deacon, "Medical Institutions of Robben Island"; Sally Swartz, "Colonialism and the Production of Psychiatric Knowledge at the Cape, 1891–1920" (Ph.D. dissertation, Univ. of Cape Town, 1996). Shula Marks is currently writing a comparative history of mental, missionary, and mine hospitals.

21. Linda Chisholm, "Reformatories and Industrial Schools in South Africa: A Study in Class, Colour, and Gender, 1882–1939" (Ph.D. dissertation, University of the Witwatersrand, 1989); Dubow, *Scientific Racism.*

22. D. Foster, "Historical and Legal Traces, 1800–1900," in *Perspectives on Mental Handicap in South Africa*, ed. Susan Lea and Don Foster (Durban: Butterworths, 1990); Dubow, *Scientific Racism,* 145–49.

23. In medical mission circles at this time, practitioners sought to combat the ubiquity of African "superstition" through biomedicine and Christianity. See Catherine Burns, "Reproductive Labors: The Politics of Women's Health in South Africa, 1900–1960" (Ph.D. dissertation, Northwestern University, 1995), chapter 7.

24. Saul Dubow, "Mental Testing and the Understanding of Race in Twentieth Century South Africa," in *Science, Medicine, and Cultural Imperialism,* ed. Teresa Meade and Mark Walker (New York: St. Martin's, 1991), 148–77; Dubow, *Scientific Racism,* chapters 4–6.

25. Vaughan, *Curing Their Ills,* 120.

26. Dubow, *Scientific Racism,* 234.

27. In an editorial in the *South African Medical Journal* 3.8 (1934), it was claimed that "the best of natives are biologically inferior to the average European." This discourse drew on an earlier racist psychiatry that had developed in the early Cape asylums. For a discussion

of the emergence of colonial psychiatry at the Cape, see Deacon, "Medical Institutions on Robben Island," chapter 4.

28. *South African Medical Journal* 3.8 (1934), cited in Vaughan, *Curing Their Ills.* See J. T. Dunston, "The Problem of the Feeble-Minded in South Africa," *Journal of Mental Science* 46 (1921): 449–58.

29. Dunston, "Problem of the Feeble-Minded," 456.

30. Ibid.

31. H. Levy, House Surgeon, to Dr. Willis, Superintendent, Pretoria Mental Hospital, 12 September 1926; "Case No. 3: Report of Raut Moleme, Msutu Female," signed by Dr. Beyers, SWH, box 8, 25/9. Without further documentation at our disposal, it is not possible to offer a satisfying explanation for such experiments nor to generalize from them.

The recourse to psychosurgery might be noted as a major innovation in Western psychiatry in the 1920s. It could raise hopes that the fatalism associated with severe mental illness might prove untrue. Psychosurgery in particular was believed to restore chronic schizophrenics to productive citizenship.

However, the precise nature of psychosurgery performed in the Non-European Hospital needs further explanation. Historians of European and British psychiatry have observed the ways in which the new sciences of gynecology and psychological medicine together revived uterine theories of hysteria and led to surgical interventions, including hysterectomy and ovariectomy and occasionally clitoridectomy. See Roy Porter, "The Body and the Mind: The Doctor and the Patient: Negotiating Hysteria," in *History of Hysteria,* ed. Roy Porter and G. Rousseau (Berkeley: University of California Press, 1992).

In a South African context, Catherine Burns's research into "Bantu gynaecology" in this period indicates that "black women . . . became the objects and, indeed subjects of wide-ranging and influential research which opened, investigated and scrutinised their bodies, and particularly their reproductive processes." She asserts that this project formed part of a wider process in which the authorities sought to regulate "the movement, settlement, productive and reproductive labour of black women." See Burns, "Reproductive Labors," chapter 9.

The links between these tendencies in medical and public policy and the operations performed at Weskoppies still need to be established. Nevertheless, it seems highly unlikely that the permission of either the women or their families were sought by the doctors for the purposes of these experiments. Moreover, the use of baboon ovaries for ovarian grafts speaks to crude evolutionist assumptions about African primitiveness.

32. McCulloch, *Colonial Psychiatry;* Vaughan, *Curing Their Ills.*

33. Colonial Secretary, Transvaal, to Colonial Secretary, Cape Colony, 5 October 1909, CS 798/12766; Physician Superintendent, Weskoppies Mental Asylum, to Assistant Colonial Secretary, 29 June 1909, CS 798/127667.

34. Sally Swartz makes these points in much of her work, but see her "Black Insane," 414–15.

35. Sachs, *Black Hamlet,* 189.

36. State parsimony and the established ideas about appropriate means of handling African mental disorder ensured that psychiatric medicine in Africa had an extremely limited reach. Many professionals and other officials considered that Africans were better treated by "their own."

37. Union of South Africa, *Report of the Commissioner of Mentally Disordered and Defective Persons for the Union of South Africa, 1919* (UG 31-'21), 5–6.

38. The phrase "great confinement" is Michel Foucault's, from his *Madness and Civilization: A History of Insanity in the Age of Reason* (New York: Pantheon Books, 1965), 38–64. Recently, however, historians have rejected the overconspiratorial portrait of psychiatric institutions as "total institutions" or agents of social control. See Catherine M. McGovern, "The Myths of Social Control and Custodial Oppression: Patterns of Psychiatric Medicine in Late Nineteenth Century Institutions," *Journal of Social History* 20.1 (1986): 3–22.

39. Chisholm, "Reformatories and Industrial Schools"; Charles van Onselen, *Studies in the Social and Economic History of the Witwatersrand, 1886–1914,* 2 vols. (Johannesburg: Ravan Press, 1982). It should be recalled, moreover, that in all these institutions—jail, asylum, and compound—it was predominantly men, rather than women, in the African population who were subjected to their disciplinary regimes. This is not surprising given that it was men who entered the domain of white employment and urban life earlier and with greater intensity than their female counterparts.

40. Inspector, Divisional CID Officer, Witwatersrand Division, to Deputy Commissioner, South African Police, Witwatersrand Division, 29 August 1920, South African Police (SAP) 6/953/23/3.

41. Elaine Showalter, *The Female Malady: Women, Madness, and English Culture, 1830–1980* (New York Pantheon Books, 1987).

42. See D. Posel, "State, Power, and Gender: Conflict over the Registration of African Customary Marriage in South Africa, c. 1910–1970," *Journal of Historical Sociology* 8.3 (1995): 222–56; Kathy Eales, "Popular Representations of Black Women on the Rand and Their Impact on the Development of Influx Controls," unpublished paper, History Workshop, University of the Witwatersrand, February 1990.

43. See for example P. Bonner, "'Desirable or Undesirable Basotho Women?' Liquor, Prostitution, and the Migration of Basotho Women to the Rand, 1920–1945," in *Women and Gender in Southern Africa to 1945*, ed. Cherryl Walker (London: James Currey, 1990), 221–50.

44. As Roy Porter has observed in the case of a seventeenth-century female prophet, Lady Eleonor Davies, who was pathologized as "mad," if she had been treated as a criminal, she might have obtained the status of a noble, brave defender of intellectual freedom, for "treason implied the possibility of truth." See Porter, "Prophetic Body."

45. See, for example, the sworn statements of Johnson Veldtman, Elliot Gara, and others in BAO 6605 11/328.

46. Secretary for Native Affairs to Native Sub-Commissioner, Pretoria, 28 January 1927, BAO 6605 11/328.

47. Personal communication, Sally Swartz to Hilary Sapire, 6 May 1997.

Bibliography

Manuscript Collections

Cape Archives Depot, Cape Town
    British Kaffraria (BK)
    East London (ELN)
State Archives Depot (SAD), Pretoria
    Colonial Secretary (CS)
    Department of Health (GES)
    Government Native Labour Bureau (GNLB)
    Justice Department (JD)
    Native Affairs Department (NTS)
    South African Police (SAP)
    Superintendent Weskoppies Mental Hospital (SWH)
University of the Witwatersrand Library
    L. F. Freed Papers

Government Publications

Cape of Good Hope. *Reports on the Government-Aided Hospitals and Invalid Homes, and Asylums for Lepers and Lunatics and Chronic-Sick Hospitals including Report of the Inspector of Lunatic Asylums for the Calendar Year 1907.* Cape Town, G41–1908.

Transvaal. *Annual Report: Public Works Department for the Year Ended 30 June 1906.* Pretoria: Government Printer, 1907.

Union of South Africa. *Annual Report of the Commissioner for Mental Hygiene.* UG 29–'27.

———. *Annual Report of the Commissioner for Mentally Disordered and Defective Persons, 1922–1923.* UG 36–'24.

———. *Commission on the Influenza Epidemic: Evidence, 1918–1919.*

———. *Report by Mr. Pienaar on Charges of Ill-Treatment Made by Ernest Francois Maas and Others against Certain Warders of the Mental Hospital at Pretoria, 1923.* A 2–'23.

———. *Report of the Commissioner of Mentally Disordered and Defective Persons for the Union of South Africa, 1919.* UG 31–'21.

———. *Report of the Mental Hospitals Departmental Committee, 1936–1937.* UG 36–'37.

———. *Report of the Select Committee on the Treatment of Lunatics.* SC 14–'13.

Secondary Sources

Abrahams, Yvette. "Disempowered to Consent: Sara Bartman and Khoisan Slavery in the Nineteenth Century Cape Colony and Britain." *South African Historical Journal* 35 (November 1996): 89–114.

Arendt, Hannah. *Eichmann in Jerusalem: A Report on the Banality of Evil.* New York: Viking, 1963.

Baines, Gary. "'In the World But Not of It': 'Bishop' Limba and the Church of Christ in New Brighton, c. 1929–1949." *Kronos* 19 (November 1992): 102–34.

Beinart, William, and Colin Bundy. *Hidden Struggles in Rural South Africa: Politics and Popular Movements in the Transkei and Eastern Cape, 1890–1930.* Johannesburg: Ravan Press, 1987.

Berger, Iris. "'Beasts of Burden' Revisited: Interpretations of Women and Gender in Southern African Societies." In *Paths Toward the Past: African Historical Essays in Honor of Jan Vansina,* ed. R. W. Harms, J. C. Miller, D. S. Newbury, and M. D. Wagner, 126–41. Atlanta: African Studies Association Press, 1994.

Bickford-Smith, Vivian. "South African Urban History, Racial Segregation, and the 'Unique' Case of Cape Town." *Journal of Southern African Studies* 21.1 (1995): 63–78.

Bozzoli, Belinda, with Mmantho Nkotsoe. *Women of Phokeng: Consciousness, Life Strategy, and Migrancy in South Africa, 1900–1983.* Johannesburg: Ravan Press, 1991.

Bradford, Helen. *A Taste Ifeedom: The ICU in Rural South Africa, 1924–1930.* New Haven: Yale University Press, 1987.

———. "'We Are Now the Men': Women's Beer Protests in the Natal Countryside, 1929." In *Class, Community, and Conflict: South African Perspectives,* ed. Belinda Bozzoli, 292–323. Johannesburg: Ravan Press, 1987.

———. "Women, Gender, and Colonialism: Rethinking the History of the British Cape Colony and Its Frontier Zones, c. 1806–1870." *Journal of African History* 27 (1996): 351–70.

Bryant, Alfred T. *Zulu Medicine and Medicine-Men.* Cape Town: C. Struik, 1966.

Bundy, Colin. *The Rise and Fall of the South African Peasantry.* Berkeley: University of California Press, 1979.

Burns, Catherine. "Reproductive Labors: The Politics of Women's Health in South Africa, 1900–1960." Ph.D. dissertation, Northwestern University, 1995.

Burns-Ncamashe, S. M. "An Investigation into the Provision of Education of the Order of Ethiopia to Africans in the Cape Province between 1900 and 1952." B.Ed. thesis, University of Cape Town, 1954.

Burrows, G. H. *A History of Medicine in South Africa up to the End of the Nineteenth Century.* Cape Town: A. A. Balkema, 1958.

Bush, Michael. *The Pilgrimage of Grace: A Study of the Rebel Armies of October 1536.* Manchester: Manchester University Press, 1996.

Butchart, Alexander. *The Anatomy of Power: European Constructions of the African Body.* London: Zed Books, 1998.

Campbell, James. *Songs of Zion: The African Methodist Episcopal Church in the United States and South Africa.* New York: Oxford University Press, 1995.

Cheetham, R. W. S., and A. Rzadkowolski. "Crosscultural Psychiatry and the Concept of Mental Illness." *South African Medical Journal* (1980): 320–25.

Chisholm, Linda. "Reformatories and Industrial Schools in South Africa: A Study in Class, Colour, and Gender, 1882–1939." Ph.D. dissertation, University of the Witwatersrand, 1989.

Clingman, Stephen. "Beyond the Limit: The Social Relations of Madness in Southern African Fiction." Unpublished paper, African Studies Institute, University of the Witwatersrand, 3 October 1988.

Cohen, David William. *The Combing of History.* Chicago: University of Chicago Press, 1994.

Comaroff, John, and Jean Comaroff. "The Madman and the Migrant." In *Ethnography and the Historical Imagination,* ed. John Comaroff and Jean Comaroff, 155–80. Boulder, Colo.: Westview Press, 1992.

A Concise English-Kaffir Dictionary. London: Longmans, Green, 1923.

Conry, J. "Insanity among Natives in the Cape Colony." *South African Medical Record* 5 (1907): 33–36.

Crais, Clifton. "Representation and the Politics of Identity in South Africa: An Eastern Cape Example." *International Journal of African Historical Studies* 25.1 (1992): 99–126.

———. *White Supremacy and Black Resistance in Pre-Industrial South Africa.* Cambridge: Cambridge University Press, 1992.

Dauskardt, R. P. A. "The Evolution of Health Systems in a Developing World Metropolis: Urban Herbalism on the Witwatersrand." M.A. thesis, University of the Witwatersrand, 1994.

Davis, W. J. *A Dictionary of the Kaffir Language Including the Xosa and Zulu Dialects.* London: Wesleyan Mission House, 1872.

Deacon, H. J. "A History of the Medical Institutions on Robben Island." Ph.D. dissertation, Cambridge University, 1994.

———. "Madness, Race, and Moral Treatment: Robben Island Lunatic Asylum, Cape Colony, 1846–1890." *History of Psychiatry* 7.2 (1996): 287–97.

de Kock, Leon. *Civilising Barbarians: Missionary Narrative and African Textual Response in Nineteenth-Century South Africa.* Johannesburg: Witwatersrand University Press, 1996.

Dennie, Garrey. "The Cultural Politics of Burial in South Africa, 1884–1990." Ph.D. dissertation, Johns Hopkins University, 1997.

Drennan, G., A. Levett, and L. Swartz. "Hidden Dimensions of Power and Resistance in the Translation Process: A South African Study." *Culture, Medicine, and Psychiatry* 15.3 (1991): 361–81.

Dubow, Saul. "Mental Testing and the Understanding of Race in Twentieth Century South Africa." In *Science, Medicine, and Cultural Imperialism*, ed. Teresa Meade and Mark Walker, 148–77. New York: St. Martin's, 1991.

———. *Scientific Racism in Modern South Africa*. Cambridge: Cambridge University Press, 1995.

Dunston, J. T. "The Problem of the Feeble-Minded in South Africa." *Journal of Mental Science* 46 (1921): 449–58.

Eales, Kathy. "Popular Representations of Black Women on the Rand and Their Impact on the Development of Influx Controls." Unpublished paper, History Workshop, University of the Witwatersrand, February 1990.

Edgar, Robert. *Because They Chose the Plan of God: The Story of the Bulhoek Massacre*. Johannesburg: Ravan Press, 1988.

———. "The Fifth Seal: Enoch Mgijima, the Israelites, and the Bullhoek Massacre." Ph.D. dissertation, University of California, Los Angeles, 1977.

———. "Garveyism in Africa: Dr. Wellington and the American Movement in the Transkei." *Ufahamu* 6.1 (1976): 31–57.

Edgar, Robert, ed. *An African American in South Africa: The Travel Notes of Ralph J. Bunche*. Athens: Ohio University Press, 1992.

Ernst, Waltraud. *Mad Tales from the Raj: The European Insane in British India, 1800–1858*. London: Routledge, 1991.

Etherington, Norman. "Recent Trends in the Historiography of Christianity in Southern Africa." *Journal of Southern African Studies* 22.2 (1996): 201–20.

Fanon, Frantz. *Black Skin, White Masks*. Trans. Charles Markmann. New York: Grove Press, 1967.

———. *The Wretched of the Earth*. Trans. Constance Farrington. New York: Grove Press, 1963.

Fast, Hildegarde. "African Perceptions of the Missionaries and Their Message: Wesleyans at Mount Coke and Butterworth, 1825–35." M.A. thesis, University of Cape Town, 1991.

———. "'In at One Ear and Out at the Other': African Responses to the Wesleyan Message in Xhosaland, 1825–1835." *Journal of Religion in Africa* 23.2 (1993): 147–74.

Feierman, Steven, and John Janzen, ed. *The Social Basis of Health and Healing in Africa.* Berkeley: University of California Press, 1992.

Fisher, A., E. Weiss, E. Mdala, and S. Tshabe. *English-Xhosa Dictionary.* Cape Town: Oxford University Press, 1985.

Foucault, Michel. *Madness and Civilization: A History of Insanity in the Age of Reason.* Trans. Richard Howard. New York: Pantheon Books, 1965.

Gaitskell, Deborah. "Devout Domesticity? A Century of African Women's Christianity in South Africa." In *Women and Gender in Southern Africa to 1945,* ed. Cherryl Walker, 251–77. London: James Currey, 1990.

———. "Power in Prayer and Service: Women's Christian Organizations." In *Christianity in South Africa: A Political, Social, and Cultural History,* ed. Richard Elphick and Rodney Davenport, 253–67. Berkeley: University of California Press, 1997.

———. "Praying and Preaching: The Distinctive Spirituality of African Women's Church Organizations." In *Missions and Christianity in South African History,* ed. Henry Bredekamp and Robert Ross, 211–32. Johannesburg: Witwatersrand University Press, 1995.

Gilman, Sander. "Black Bodies, White Bodies: Towards an Iconography of Female Sexuality in Late Nineteenth Century Art, Medicine, and Literature." In *"Race," Writing, and Difference,* ed. Henry Louis Gates, 223–61. Chicago: University of Chicago Press, 1986.

Goffman, Erving. *Asylums: Essays on the Social Situation of Mental Patients and Other Inmates.* Garden City, N.Y.: Anchor Books, 1961.

Gould, Stephen Jay. *The Flamingo's Smile: Reflections in Natural History.* New York: Norton, 1985.

Greenlees, T. D. "Insanity among the Natives in the Cape Colony." *Journal of Mental Science* 41 (1895): 71–81.

Grundlingh, Albert, and Hilary Sapire. "From Feverish Festival to Repetitive Ritual? The Changing Fortunes of 'Great Trek' Mythology in an Industrialising South Africa." *South African Historical Journal* 21 (1989): 19–38.

Gunner, Liz. "Mothers, Daughters, and Madness in the Work by Four Women Writers: Bessie Head, Jean Rhys, Ama Ata Aidoo, and Tsitsi Dangarembga." Unpublished paper, n.d.

Hammond-Tooke, W. D. *Rituals and Medicines: Indigenous Healing in South Africa.* Johannesburg: Ad. Donker, 1989.

Hare, E. "The Two Manias: A Study of the Evolution of the Modern Concept of Mania." *British Journal of Psychiatry* 88 (1981): 289–96.

Harries, Patrick. *Work, Culture, and Identity: Migrant Laborers in Mozambique and South Africa, c. 1860–1910.* Portsmouth, N.H.: Heinemann, 1994.

Head, Bessie. *A Question of Power.* London: Heinemann, 1974.

Hefner, Robert, ed. *Conversion to Christianity: Historical and Anthropological Perspectives on a Great Transformation.* Berkeley: University of California Press, 1993.

Henderson, D. K., and R. D. Gillespie. *A Textbook of Psychiatry for Students and Practitioners.* Oxford: Oxford University Press, 1927.

Hirst, Manton. "A River of Metaphors: Interpreting the Xhosa Diviner's Myth." In *Culture and the Commonplace: Anthropological Essays in Honour of David Hammond-Tooke,* ed. Patrick McAllister, 217–50. Johannesburg: Witwatersrand University Press, 1997.

Hodgson, Janet. "Ntsikana: History and Symbol: Studies in a Process of Religious Change among Xhosa-Speaking People." Ph.D. dissertation, University of Cape Town, 1985.

———. *Ntsikana's "Great Hymn": A Xhosa Expression of Christianity in the Early Nineteenth Century Eastern Cape.* Rondebosch: Centre for African Studies, University of Cape Town, 1980.

Jackson, Lynette. "Gender and Disorder and the Colonial Psychiatric Wards: A Look at the Experience of Mad Black Women in Colonial Southern Rhodesia." Paper presented to the history department seminar, University of Zimbabwe, 19 August 1992.

Janzen, John M., with William Arkinstall. *The Quest for Therapy in Lower Zaire: Medical Pluralism in Lower Zaire.* Berkeley: University of California Press, 1978.

Junod, Henri Phillipe. *Revenge or Reformation? A Study of the South African Prison System with Special Reference to Africans.* Christian Council Study Series. Lovedale: Lovedale Press, 1944.

Kennedy, D. "The Perils of the Midday Sun: Climatic Anxieties in the Colonial Tropics." In *The Empire of Nature: Hunting, Conservation, and British Imperialism,* ed. John MacKenzie, 118–40. Manchester: Manchester University Press, 1988.

Kruger, Albert. *Mental Health Law in South Africa.* Durban: Butterworths, 1980.

Laubscher, B. J. F. *Sex, Custom, and Psychopathology: A Study of South African Pagan Natives.* London: Routledge, 1937.

Lea, Susan, and Don Foster, eds. *Perspectives on Mental Handicap in South Africa.* Durban: Butterworths, 1990.

Lewis, I. M. *Ecstatic Religion: An Anthropological Study of Spirit Possession and Shamanism.* Harmondsworth: Penguin Books, 1971.

Lipsedge, M. "Religion and Madness in History." In *Psychiatry and Religion: Context, Consensus, and Controversies,* ed. Dinesh Bhugra, 23–47. London: Routledge, 1995.

Longmore, Laura. *The Dispossessed: A Study of the Sex-Life of Bantu Women in Urban Areas in and around Johannesburg.* London: Corgi Books, 1959.

Lonsdale, John. "The Prayers of Waikyaki: Political Uses of the Kikuyu Past." In *Revealing Prophets: Prophecy in Eastern African History,* ed. David Anderson and Douglas Johnson, 240–91. Athens: Ohio University Press, 1995.

Mager, Anne. "Gender and the Making of the Ciskei, 1945–1959." Ph.D. dissertation, University of Cape Town, 1995.

Manganyi, C. "Making Strange: Race Science and Ethnopsychiatric Discourse." Paper presented to the African Studies Institute seminar, University of the Witwatersrand, 15 October 1984.

Marks, Shula. "The Context of Personal Narrative: Reflections on 'Not Either an Experimental Doll': The Separate Worlds of Three South African Women." In *Interpreting Women's Lives: Feminist Theory and Personal Narratives,* ed. Personal Narrative Group, 39–55. Bloomington: Indiana University Press, 1989.

———. *'Not Either an Experimental Doll': The Separate Worlds of Three South African Women.* London: Women's Press, 1987.

————.'*Not Either an Experimental Doll': The Separate Worlds of Three South African Women:* Ten Years On." Paper presented to the Gender in Empire and Commonwealth, Societies of Southern Africa joint seminar, Institute of Commonwealth Studies, London, 16 October 1997.

————. "Rewriting South African History; or, the Hunt for Hintsa's Head." Seventh Annual Bindoff Lecture, Queen Mary and Westfield College, University of London, 12 March 1996.

Marks, Shula, ed. *'Not Either an Experimental Doll': The Separate Worlds of Three South African Women.* London: Women's Press, 1987.

Mayer, Philip. "The Origin and Decline of Two Rural Resistance Ideologies." In *Black Villagers in an Industrial Society: Anthropological Perspectives on Labour Migration in South Africa,* ed. Philip Mayer, 1–80. Cape Town: Oxford University Press, 1980.

————. *Socialization: The Approach from Social Anthropology.* New York: Tavistock, 1970.

Mayer, Philip, with Iona Mayer. *Townsmen or Tribesmen: Conservatism and the Process of Urbanization in a South African City.* Cape Town: Oxford University Press, 1961.

McCulloch, Jock. *Colonial Psychiatry and "the African Mind."* Cambridge: Cambridge University Press, 1995.

————. "The Emperor's New Clothes: Ethnopsychiatry in Colonial Africa." *History of the Human Sciences* 6.2 (1993): 35–52.

McGovern, Catherine M. "The Myths of Social Control and Custodial Oppression: Patterns of Psychiatric Medicine in Late Nineteenth Century Institutions." *Journal of Social History* 20.1 (1986): 3–22.

Micale, Mark. "Hysteria and Its Historiography." Part 1. *History of Science* 27.3 (1989): 223–61.

Minde, M. "History of Mental Health Services in South Africa." Part 3, "Cape Province." *South African Medical Journal* 48 (1974): 2230–34.

————. "History of Mental Health Services in South Africa." Part 7, "Services since Union." *South African Medical Journal* 49.11 (1975): 405–9.

Moodie, T. Dunbar, with Vivienne Ndatshe. *Going for Gold: Men,*

Mines, and Migration. Los Angeles: University of California Press, 1994.

Mouton, F. A. *Voices in the Desert: Margaret and William Ballinger, A Biography*. Pretoria: Benedic Books, 1997.

Ngubane, Harriet. *Body and Mind in Zulu Medicine*. New York: Academic Press, 1977.

―――. "Clinical Practice and Organization of Indigenous Healers in South Africa." *Social Science and Medicine* 15B (1981): 361–66.

―――. "Spirit Possession in Zulu Cosmology." In *Religion and Social Change in Southern Africa*, ed. Michael Whisson and Martin West, 48–57. Cape Town: David Philip, 1975.

Nuttall, Sarah and Carli Coetzee, eds. *Negotiating the Past: The Making of Memory in South Africa*. Cape Town: Oxford University Press, 1998.

Olivier, A. J. "Weskoppies Hospitaal, 1891–1966." Unpublished paper, n.d.

Oosthuizen, Gerhardus. *The Healer-Prophet in Afro-Christian Churches*. Leiden: E. J. Brill, 1992.

Opland, Jeff. "Nontsoza Ngqwetho: Xhosa Woman Newspaper Poet of the 1920s." Paper presented to the seminar Gender in Empire and Commonwealth, Institute of Commonwealth Studies, London, 3 November 1994.

Pauw, B. A. "Universalism and Particularism in the Beliefs of Xhosa-speaking Christians." In *Religion and Social Change in Southern Africa*, ed. Michael Whisson and Martin West, 153–63. Cape Town: David Philip, 1975.

―――. *Christianity and Xhosa Tradition: Belief and Ritual among Xhosa-Speaking Christians*. New York: Oxford University Press, 1975.

Peires, J. B. *The Dead Will Arise: Nongqawuse and the Great Xhosa Cattle-Killing Movement of 1856–57*. Bloomington: Indiana University Press, 1989.

―――. *The House of Phalo: A History of the Xhosa People in the Days of Their Independence*. Johannesburg: Ravan Press, 1981.

Phillips, Howard. *"Black October": The Impact of the Spanish Influenza Epidemic of 1918 on South Africa*. Archives Year Book for South African History. Pretoria: Government Printer, 1990.

Phillips, Ray E. *The Bantu in the City: A Study of Cultural Adjustment on the Witwatersrand.* Lovedale: Lovedale Press, 1938.

Plug, C., and J. L. Roos. "Weskoppies Hospital, Founded 1892: The Early Years." *South African Medical Journal* 81 (1992): 218–21.

Porter, Roy. "The Body and the Mind: The Doctor and the Patient: Negotiating Hysteria," In *History of Hysteria,* ed. Roy Porter and G. Rousseau. Berkeley: University of California Press, 1992.

———. *Mind-Forg'd Manacles: A History of Madness in England from the Restoration to the Regency.* London: Athlone Press, 1987.

———. "The Prophetic Body: Lady Eleonor Davies and the Meanings of Madness." *Women's Writing* 1 (1994): 51–54.

Posel, D. "State, Power, and Gender: Conflict over the Registration of African Customary Marriage in South Africa, c. 1910–1970." *Journal of Historical Sociology* 8.3 (1995): 222–56.

Ramphele, Mamphela. "Political Widowhood in South Africa: The Embodiment of Ambiguity." *Daedalus* 125.1 (1996): 99–118.

Ranger, T. O. "The Influenza Pandemic in Southern Rhodesia: A Crisis of Comprehension." In *Imperial Medicine and Indigenous Societies,* ed. David A. Arnold, 172–89. New York: St. Martin's, 1988.

———. "Plagues of Beasts and Men: Prophetic Responses to Epidemic in Eastern and Southern Africa." In *Epidemics and Ideas: Essays on the Historical Perception of Pestilence,* ed. T. O. Ranger and Paul Slack, 241–68. Cambridge: Cambridge University Press, 1992.

Rassool, Ciraj, and Leslie Witz. "The 1952 Jan van Riebeeck Tercentenary Festival: Constructing and Contesting Public National History in South Africa." *Journal of African History* 34 (1993): 447–68.

Sachs, Wulf. *Black Hamlet: The Mind of an African Negro Revealed by Psychoanalysis.* London: Geoffrey Bles, 1937.

Sadowsky, Jonathan. "The Confinements of Isaac O: A Case of 'Acute Mania' in Colonial Nigeria." *History of Psychiatry* 7.1 (1996): 91–112.

———. *Imperial Bedlam: Institutions of Madness in Colonial Southwest Nigeria.* Berkeley: University of California Press, 1999.

———. "Insanity and the Problem of Hegemony: 'Cases' from Colonial Nigeria." Paper presented to the Department of Anthropology, University of the Witwatersrand, 1995.

Scheff, Thomas J. *Being Mentally Ill: A Sociological Theory.* Chicago: Aldine, 1966.

Scheub, Harold. "And So I Grew Up: The Autobiography of Nongenile Masithathu Zenani." In *Life Histories of African Women,* ed. Patricia W. Romero, 7–45. Atlantic Highlands, N.J.: Ashfield Press, 1988.

Scull, Andrew. *The Most Solitary of Afflictions: Madness and Society in Britain, 1700–1900.* New Haven: Yale University Press, 1993.

———. "Psychiatry and Social Control in the Nineteenth and Twentieth Centuries." *History of Psychiatry* 2.2 (1991): 149–69.

Searle, Charlotte. *The History of the Development of Nursing in South Africa, 1652–1960: A Socio-Historical Survey.* Pretoria: South African Nursing Association, 1965, 1980.

Showalter, Elaine. *The Female Malady: Women, Madness, and English Culture, 1830–1980.* New York: Pantheon Books, 1985.

Soga, John H. *The Ama-Xosa: Life and Customs.* Lovedale: Lovedale Press, 1931.

Stoler, Ann, and Frederick Cooper, eds. *Tensions of Empire: Colonial Cultures in a Bourgeois World.* Berkeley: University of California Press, 1997.

Sundkler, Bengt. "African Church History in a New Key." In *Religion, Development, and African Identity,* ed. Kirsten Petersen, 73–84. Uppsala: Scandinavian Institute of African Studies, 1987.

———. *Bantu Prophets in South Africa.* 2d ed. London: Oxford University Press, 1961.

———. *The Christian Ministry in Africa.* Uppsala: Swedish Institute of Missionary Research, 1960.

Swanson, Felicity. "Colonial Madness: The Construction of Gender in the Grahamstown Lunatic Asylum, 1875–1905." B.A. (Honours) thesis, University of Cape Town, 1994.

Swartz, Leslie. *Culture and Mental Health: A Southern African View.* Cape Town: Oxford University Press, 1998.

———. "Issues for Cross Cultural Psychiatric Research in South Africa." *Culture, Medicine, and Psychiatry* 9.1 (1985): 59–74.

Swartz, Sally. "The Black Insane in the Cape, 1891–1920." *Journal of Southern African Studies* 21.3 (1995): 399–416.

———. "Changing Diagnoses in Valkenberg Asylum, Cape Colony, 1891–1920: A Longitudinal View." *History of Psychiatry* 6.4 (1995): 431–51.

———. "Colonialism and the Production of Psychiatric Knowledge in the Cape, 1891–1920." Ph.D. dissertation, University of Cape Town, 1996.

———. "Colonizing the Insane: Causes of Insanity in the Cape, 1891–1920." *History of the Human Sciences* 8.4 (1995): 39–57.

Switzer, Les. *Power and Resistance in an African Society: The Ciskei Xhosa and the Making of South Africa.* Madison: University of Wisconsin Press, 1993.

Turrell, Robert. "Hanging Women: The 'Singular Case' of Mietje Bontnaal." Paper presented to the Societies of Southern Africa seminar, Institute of Commonwealth Studies, London, 25 April 1998.

van Onselen, Charles. "Dead but Not Quite Buried." *London Review of Books* 20.21 (29 October 1998): 23–24.

———. *Studies in the Social and Economic History of the Witwatersrand, 1886–1914.* 2 vols. Johannesburg: Ravan Press, 1982.

Vaughan, Megan. *Curing Their Ills: Colonial Power and African Illness.* London: Polity Press, 1991.

———. "Idioms of Madness: Zomba Lunatic Asylum, Nyasaland in the Colonial Period." *Journal of Southern African Studies* 9.2 (1983): 218–38.

———. "Madness and Colonialism, Colonialism as Madness: Re-Reading Fanon, Colonial Discourse Theory, Fanon, and the Psychopathology of Colonialism." Paper presented to the Association of African Studies of the United Kingdom, Stirling University, September 1992.

Walker, Cherryl. "Gender and the Development of the Migrant Labour System, c. 1850–1930." In *Women and Gender in Southern Africa to 1945*, ed. Cherryl Walker, 168–97. London: James Currey, 1990.

Walker, Cherryl, ed. *Women and Gender in Southern Africa to 1945.* London: James Currey, 1990.

Walker, Sheila. *The Religious Revolution in the Ivory Coast: The Prophet Harris and the Harrist Church.* Chapel Hill: University of North Carolina Press, 1983.

Walls, Andrew. *The Missionary Movement in Christian History: Studies in the Transmission of Faith.* Maryknoll, N.Y.: Orbis Books, 1996.

West, Martin. *Bishops and Prophets in a Black City: African Independent Churches in Soweto, Johannesburg.* Cape Town: David Philip, 1975.

Willan, Brian. "An African in Kimberley: Sol T. Plaatje, 1894–1898." In *Industrialization and Social Change in South Africa,* ed. Shula Marks and Richard Rathbone, 238–58. London: Longman, 1982.

Wilson, Monica Hunter. *Reaction to Conquest: Effects of Contact with Europeans on the Pondo of South Africa.* 2d ed. London: Oxford University Press, 1961.

Wilson, Monica Hunter, and Leonard Thompson, eds. *Oxford History of South Africa.* 2 vols. Vol. 2: *South Africa, 1870–1966.* Oxford: Oxford University Press, 1971.

Index